Blue
is the Color

*George and Marian —
Thank you for the
gift of your prayers
and encouragement
over so many years!
with love,
Anne*

Blue is the Color

and Other Stories of Uncommon Grace

Anne Childs

Peregrini Press – Llantwit Major, Wales

Blue is the Color and Other Stories of Uncommon Grace

Copyright © 2018 Peregrini Press. All rights reserved.

ISBN: 1-99-960791-0

ISBN-978-1-99-960791-3

No part of this book shall be reproduced or transmitted in any form or by any means, electronic or mechanical, including photocopying, recording, or by any information retrieval system without written permission of the publisher – except for brief quotations for the purpose of news, review or scholarship.

Illustrations by Alice Paschal and Christine Riker.

Published by Peregrini Press, a division of Awen Collaborative Limited

For inquiries related to this book please email: info@peregrinipress.com or call Tel: +44-(0)7597-170650

Unless otherwise noted, scripture quotations are taken from the Holy Bible, New International Version, copyright © 1996, 2004, 2007 by Tyndale House Foundation. Used by permission of Tyndale House Publishers, Inc., Carol Stream, Illinois 60188. All rights reserved.

Every effort has been made to make this book as complete and as accurate as possible, but no warranty of fitness is implied. The information is provided on an "as is" basis. The author and the publisher shall have neither liability nor responsibility to any person or entity with respect to any loss or damages arising from the information contained in this book.

DEDICATION

To John, Kristen, Andrea, and Luke
because we did this together
and
to our co-workers and friends
who have spent a lifetime among the Tarahumara
doing medical work, community development, literacy,
Bible translation and many other acts of service.
Your sacrifice has not gone unnoticed.

TABLE OF CONTENTS

Miles and Light Years	1
When Words Fail	3
Yellow Gloves	7
Ears to Hear	11
A Hardscrabble World	15
Making Sense of Things	17
Beauty in a Brown Paper Bag	21
Old Jake	25
Samuel's Question	29
Of Cows and Clothes	33
All Things New	37
What About Christmas?	41
Chicken Soup	45
Solitary Labor	49
Such as These	53
Casi Mira	57
Mice in the Middle of the Night	61
A Glad Welcome	63
A Dilemma of Choice	67
Conspiracy of the Common	71
When God is Silent	75
Cricket Song	77
Some Things Stay with You Forever	81
Sheer Extravagance	85
Loving the Unlovely	87
Blue is the Color	91
A Two Lepta Life	97
I Won't Be Here When You Get Back	101
Everything about Everything	105
Our Times Are in His Hands	109
A Final Prayer of Desperate Faith	113
About the Author	115
Books from Peregrini Press	117

For from his fullness we have all received, grace upon grace.

John 1:16 (ESV)

MILES AND LIGHT YEARS

Two thousand miles from home and light years from anything even vaguely familiar, our Ram Charger inched down a steep hill, and the valley, perched at 8000 feet, opened before us. We caught a glimpse of the isolated community where we were to live. I climbed out to unlatch a simple gate that marked the entrance to the Tarahumara community and closed it after John drove through. Our three children, Luke, Andrea, and Kristen, ages 4-10, sat wide-eyed and eager.

We had covered vast amounts of unfamiliar terrain to arrive at this place, including John's studies in Development Anthropology, a year of Spanish language school, and introductory classes in Tarahumara culture and language. Everything we thought we'd need for a radically different lifestyle was packed into boxes wedged in or tied on top of the vehicle. After years of preparation and two days driving south of the U.S./Mexico border, the last two and a half hours of the journey left no doubt we had crossed an invisible boundary and found ourselves in a strange world.

As we bumped slowly along the hard-packed dirt road that wound through the center of the miles-long valley, we all grew silent. We rolled down the windows to let it all in, and as much felt as saw the scenes unfolding before us. It was stunning. The autumn afternoon was warm, with a high-elevation, crystalline blue sky. The cornfields, now dry and rattling in the breeze, came often to the very edge of the road, and flowed up and down the hillsides. Small log houses dotted the fields, wispy smoke floating from the chimneys of some. A flock of sheep ranged freely on a far slope, the ringing of their bells and their faint bleating carried on the wind. And scattered throughout all the bronze, earthy colors of this landscape were the brilliant reds, blues, and greens of the Tarahumara women in their wonderfully vivid dresses.

What follows is a collection of encounters—some commonplace, some remarkable—in this, our new home. They are accounts of bumping into God. About arriving at some far-flung location and discovering His footprints everywhere.

Mostly these are stories about revelation. Mine.

I'm not a theologian, only a story-teller. But in these pages I hope you see the everywhere-present Kingdom and its ever gracious King.

~ Anne Childs

WHEN WORDS FAIL

During supper one evening our neighbor Samuel ran to our door screaming, "Rojelio is dead! Rojelio is dead! Down in the *arroyo*!"

We knew Rojelio, his mentally handicapped 24-year-old brother, as a gentle, quiet young man, seemingly happy in spite of his limitations. He lived with his parents, our closest neighbors.

Stunned, we ran after Samuel to the edge of the ravine where the ground dropped to the stream below. We picked our way carefully down the rocky slope, and there Rojelio lay, drowned in just a few inches of water after suffering an apparent seizure while bathing.

As other family members gathered, I hurried back to our house for a sheet to cover the body. After the arrival of Roberto and Rosa, Rojelio's parents, three male family members and John laid the body in the sheet, and, each taking a corner, carried it out of the arroyo to the family home.

Since our house was just a stone's throw from theirs, we had a close-up view of how the family mourned. All night a fire blazed outside their house. Family and friends huddled in its warmth and talked in muffled voices. Other relatives kept a candlelight vigil in the kitchen next to the body, which was stretched out on a cot in the middle of the dirt floor. In a culture with no funeral homes or undertakers, the business of death was handled entirely by the family. Everything was centered in the home. The place where they had first received and welcomed Rojelio as a newborn baby was now the place from which they bid him farewell.

In the morning John and another man fashioned a coffin from some pine boards we had stored behind our house. Curly shavings of clean pine dropped to the ground as the men took turns sliding the hand plane back and forth over the rough boards. Then they cut the smooth yellow planks with hand saws and hammered the pieces into a simple box. While the coffin was being made, two of Rojelio's brothers and a cousin walked to the cemetery at the upper end of the valley and dug the grave by hand.

We did not see the family place Rojelio's body in the coffin, nor did we observe the finality of nails being driven into the lid. Only those closest to Rojelio bore witness to those stark realities.

Early that afternoon family and friends crowded into the dirt yard in front of Roberto and Rosa's mud-brick house, and a brief memorial service was held, with Alfredo, a cousin, officiating. Afterward everyone piled into the few trucks available and we all headed to the cemetery. I was astonished at how many people trickled in on foot from all directions. The lack of phone service did not stop the news from traveling rapidly through the mountain grapevine, and people from the entire length of the valley appeared at the cemetery.

Three ropes were passed under the coffin. Six men stepped up and, each holding a rope end, they lowered the box into the ground. We all walked slowly past the grave, picked up a handful of earth, and gently tossed it in. Finally, as the crowd circled back around the gaping hole, several men picked up shovels and began moving dirt into the grave. When Roberto picked up a shovel and began laboring to bury his own son, I fought to hold back tears. In any culture, it's not supposed to be this way. Parents should never bury their children.

Early that evening, I carried a steaming pot of pinto beans and a loaf of homemade bread to the family. Kristen brought a coffeecake she had made. As we stepped into their kitchen bearing our simple gifts two feelings washed over me.

One, gathered from the silence that fell upon the room as we entered, was a sense of being an outsider, an awkward one who, despite good intentions, still knew very little of the ways and thoughts of these people. I hadn't noticed anyone else bringing food. Was it even considered appropriate? I had no idea how the Tarahumara expressed shared grief.

The second feeling was one of simply being part of the human family, a fellow sufferer of the universal pain that accompanies death.

With a few feeble words of explanation we handed over the food we carried. They received our offerings with no show of emotion, and as we stepped back through the door and walked home in silence, I lamented my lack of words and inability to express the deep sadness I felt.

Early the next day we heard a rhythmic thunk …thunk …thunk and were surprised to discover Roberto at our back door, unloading firewood from a heavily burdened donkey. When we began to thank him he just nodded and lifted his hand to silence us. I realized he wanted no words, that no words were necessary. Twice more that day, Roberto and his donkey blessed us with more firewood, which was added wordlessly to the pile by the back door.

And so we received his silent gift, recognizing it as an expression of appreciation and commonality. Even though we had fumbled our way through his family's tragedy, unsure what to do or say, somehow, aided by a mysterious common language, our hearts had been heard.

……

"…weep with them that weep."
Romans 12:15 (KJV)

YELLOW GLOVES

On a bitter day, with wind whipping dirt into swirls that periodically enveloped us, I set out on foot with my children and a bundle of dirty clothes. My destination: the stream that wound through the valley; my goal: to wash our clothes before the temperature dropped further. It wasn't long before the kids gave up and headed back to the warmth of the wood-burning stove in our small cabin. Alone with a mound of dirty clothing, I wrestled as much with God as with my task.

Kneeling in the sand, I plunged a t-shirt into the trickle of cold water, my frustration silently spilling out. *Just want You to know this isn't working, God. I don't fit in here!* I spread the wet shirt on a smooth rock and rubbed the bar of laundry soap over it, then gathered it into a loose ball, scooped a little water from the stream, and squeezed and rubbed the fabric until a nice lather formed. *I'm sick of being laughed at. Who cares if I don't know how to grind corn, can't make round tortillas, never killed a chicken?* I moved the shirt across the rock in a rhythm I had seen the Tarahumara women use. Scrub, scrub, scrub, turn. Scrub, scrub, scrub, turn. *Nobody even cares about the things I'm good at. What a mistake to send me here!*

Tears stung my eyes, so I leaned back on my heels to compose myself, my hands aching from the icy water. After warming my hands in my jacket pockets, I reluctantly got out some yellow rubber gloves and pulled them on. There was no way I could wash the pile of laundry at my side unless I wore those gloves, but I dreaded the thought of being seen and laughed at one more time.

I bent again to my task and allowed my silent protests to continue. After a while I looked downstream and saw a Tarahumara woman in a traditional red pleated skirt and blouse making her way along the path in my direction. I groaned inwardly and scrubbed harder, hoping to look so occupied that she'd dare not interrupt. Surely she would branch off on another path. I glanced again quickly. She was still approaching. In another moment I could tell she was heading directly to me.

I stood and tried to peel the hideous yellow gloves from my hands, but water had gotten inside, and the more I tugged at them, the stronger became the suction that held them in place. Finally, she stood before me, hand outstretched in greeting. Mortified, I offered my yellow-gloved hand, waiting to see her left hand move to cover her mouth, a Tarahumara expression of embarrassment or amusement.

Her right hand lightly touched my yellow glove in a typical Tarahumara handshake, but her left hand never moved. She didn't laugh. She had a strikingly beautiful face, deeply lined and weathered, but bearing unusually fine features and sensitive eyes. She spoke no Spanish, and I spoke limited Tarahumara, so after I used up just about every word I knew we smiled awkwardly at one another for a few moments and then she made motions to leave.

She headed toward the path on my left and I dropped again to my knees by the water, relieved that the encounter was over. Instead of walking away, however, she circled behind me and to my astonishment knelt next to me in the sand on my right.

One after another, she picked up my family's soiled socks and scrubbed them clean again. She worked in silence, smiling shyly at the surprise and gratitude I struggled to express as I finished washing the dirty t-shirts. When at last she added the final sock to the small mountain of clean ones she had completed, she got to her feet. I did too. And this time I offered my yellow-gloved hand without fear of ridicule. "*Ma te teraba*," I said, thanking her in Tarahumara. As she turned and continued down the path, I prayed a silent prayer over her, doubting she had any idea how she had blessed me.

I never saw the woman again nor did I discover who she was. But this much I knew: She was a grace-gift to me, evidence of the heavenly moving among those rooted to earth.

I know such gifts rain down around me with frequency, big drops landing on the dry soil of my existence, sparkling on my landscapes, evidencing a reality that challenges my notions. Some gifts are plain and ordinary; others, like that Tarahumara woman, are outrageous enough to suck my breath away. The problem is that I often plod with eyes to the ground, intent only on my own two feet and where they are taking me. I fail to lift my face to the shower of grace falling all around me.

God blessed me profoundly that day. He used an unknown woman who spoke barely a word, but whose simple actions called down a message of Kingdom reality when I was desperate for it. In doing so He provided far more than mere assistance on laundry day. He demonstrated the gracious humanity of the people I'd come to live among, He lavished on me a good dose of unconditional love, and He assured me that no, He hadn't made a mistake when He sent me there.

......

"The earth is the Lord's, and everything in it, the world,
and all who live in it…" Psalm 24:1

EARS TO HEAR

While chatting in the sun one afternoon with Martina she abruptly announced, "Here comes Juan." I shot her a puzzled look. John had driven off to town that morning and, with six hours travel time on top of his errands, I didn't expect him back until late afternoon. She caught my look and threw back her head, laughing.

Not wanting to make an issue of her confusion, I said simply, "He's in Creel today."

We resumed our conversation, and she elaborated on her certainty that the newly-elected traditional governor would soon be helping himself to community money. After a minute or so I heard the distant rumble of a vehicle but thought nothing of it. The noise gradually became louder, until I knew it was slowly crossing the *arroyo* and climbing the last rise that opened onto our section of the valley. When our Ram Charger crested the hill and began picking its way down the rocky slope toward us, I looked at Martina as if she had clairvoyant powers. "How did you know?" I asked.

Her eyes crinkled as she laughed at me again. "I could hear him," she said.

This scenario happened over and over again. Any time John drove off somewhere, my neighbors were aware of his imminent return before I was. They could even distinguish between the sound of our vehicle and one of the three or four other trucks in the valley. John, too, had experiences of being clueless when neighbors could hear a vehicle approaching.

We quickly realized their powers of hearing were superior to ours and attributed it to two things: Televisions, music, washing machines, dryers, and the drone of traffic filled the world we came from. The Tarahumara sense of hearing had not been deadened by this constant barrage of noise. In addition, Tarahumara ears were surrounded by sounds purely natural to the environment—birds singing, donkeys braying, roosters crowing. Anything mechanical or unnatural stood out to them immediately.

My diminished ability to hear distant sounds shocked me. I'd never had anything to compare myself to before and now I was coming up short.

Jesus often challenged His listeners' ability to discern the subtle truth inherent in His words. "He who has ears to hear, let him hear," He would say. What is divinely clear is often muddled by human reason. Plain and simple truth can be hard for us to hear.

But beyond this inability to hear and receive the words of Jesus, I also evidence another sort of hearing loss.

There is recorded evidence of a great chorus, celestial and terrestrial, filling the world in which we live. When the very foundations of earth were being laid and our world in all its wonder was being created, "…the morning stars sang together and all the angels shouted for joy." The sound waves created when those songs and shouts first rent the air still reverberate throughout our earth. The pure joy expressed in those responses to God's work still permeates our world. *He who has ears to hear, let him hear.*

In a great reorienting of Job's (and our) understanding God asks: "Have you ever given orders to the morning, or shown the dawn its place? Have you entered the storehouses of the snow? What is the way to the place where the east winds are scattered over the earth? Who gives birth to the frost from the heavens? Can you bring forth the constellations in their seasons or lead out the Bear with her cubs? Does the hawk take flight by your wisdom?" We are surrounded by a constant, nonverbal declaration of the nature and power of God, which we can either attend to or ignore. *He who has ears to hear, let him hear.*

Scripture also offers varied glimpses into the joyous anthem which accompanies our daily lives. We read that the heavens sing for joy, the earth shouts aloud and rejoices, the mountains and forests burst into song, and the trees of the field clap their hands. Creation cannot remain silent; it is both stage and choir in the most jubilant of concerts. Its holy, happy noise attests without ceasing to the greatness of our God and His incomprehensible purposes for His world. *He who has ears to hear, let him hear.*

I can be late to hear an approaching vehicle bouncing along the dirt road and it impacts my life little. However, to grow oblivious to the ever-present proclamation of God's magnificent activity in my midst leaves me diminished, impoverished, hardened. Even when it is silent our world never ceases to speak. Even when we turn a deaf ear a great chorus of praise envelopes us.

Listen! I hear the beautiful strains of an ancient song.

Do you?

......

"The heavens declare the glory of God;
the skies proclaim the work of his hands.
Day after day they pour forth speech;
night after night they display knowledge.
There is no speech or language where their voice is not heard.
Their voice goes out into all the earth,
their words to the ends of the world."
Psalm 19:1-4

A HARDSCRABBLE WORLD

As I settled myself on a crude plank bench in the log church building, the familiar smell of the people—a mingled fragrance of sweat and wood smoke—enveloped me. It was a distinctly Tarahumara smell—not offensive, just unique—to me as much a part of the culture as their colorful clothing.

Tarahumara women in bright, heavily pleated skirts and blouses, wearing slip-on plastic shoes, lined the benches and covered the floor of one side of the room. Babies were secured to their backs with multicolored shawls. Children snuggled on their laps or at their feet on the cement floor.

On the other side of the room, men sat or stood against the log walls. Most wore tattered jeans with long-sleeved plaid shirts and old tennis shoes or handmade huarache sandals. The occasional more traditional man wore a loincloth. New Jesus-followers and seekers alike crammed into the relative warmth of the unheated room on this chilly day.

Dogs wandered slyly in, reveling in their breach of security, until someone whispered loudly, "chooo-cho!" and shooed them, tails tucked, toward the open door. Babies whimpered and some people talked in hushed voices, while most seemed content to sit in companionable silence waiting for the service to begin.

Just then a man walked in and settled himself on a rough bench along the left front wall. It was José Luís, a Tarahumara man in his thirties who had a blind wife and several children. He sat unpretentiously but very straight, and with a quiet pride. It was then I noticed his clothes.

He had somehow come upon some new used clothing and was wearing a long-sleeved dress shirt, yellow with white pin stripes and a white collar. The top two buttons were open, and a bright red paisley tie was loosely knotted around his neck and hung at a crooked angle down the front of the shirt. He had on jeans that were several inches too short and had a large bleach stain on one leg. The ensemble was completed by an orange baseball cap and a pair of cowboy boots. With his large, tortoiseshell glasses he formed an astonishing figure.

As the off-key Ranchero-style music started and everyone clapped to the beat of his own drummer, I could not keep my eyes off José Luís. He sang, he clapped, he looked remarkably dignified in his own world. And I was flooded with three conflicting emotions.

One was great pride. He wore his very best that day and he knew it. I knew it too.

The second was a large dose of amusement. No matter how I approached it, the total effect was comical.

The third was sadness, a deep ache of regret that this was likely the best he'll ever know. L.L. Bean, J. C. Penney, and even Walmart were from another planet, unknown, irrelevant offerings in his hardscrabble world. A troubling awareness settled over me. His finest will always be someone else's cast-offs.

When the Tarahumara pastor got up to speak, it mattered little that I could not understand his words. The message for me that day rang loud and clear. It was a message that superseded language and leaped across cultural barriers, landing, ultimately, right in my lap: To whom much is given, much will be required.

......

> "Much is required from those to whom much is given,
> for their responsibility is greater." Luke 12:48 (TLB)

MAKING SENSE OF THINGS

I gripped the armrests and pressed one knee into the door to stabilize myself against the pitching motion of our Ram Charger as it lurched over a series of huge potholes. Fueling my nausea, odors of stale sweat and urine floated from the backseat where Paulino and his wife sat with their undiapered baby. The pungent scent of their smoke-saturated clothing added yet another layer to the fragrance frenzy that filled the car and was wreaking havoc with my weak stomach. It didn't help that our five-person vehicle was carrying eight; we were all shoe-horned in, with Kristen and Andrea wedged into the backseat with our guests and Luke squeezed in next to me on the front bucket seat.

When, after two and a half hours, we reached the paved road I took a deep breath and let it out slowly, an attempt to purge the queasiness and relax my vigilant muscles. Now that clouds of dust from the dirt roads no longer enveloped us, we opened the windows, and I took big gulps of fresh air while enjoying the last thirty minutes of travel.

Getting to town was an ordeal, but once there I enjoyed what luxuries a small Mexican mountain community could offer. We would restock on groceries, let the kids spend a few *pesos* on treasures at one of the variety stores, and enjoy lunch at Lupita's café before turning around and retracing all those grueling miles back to the village.

On this day, as was often the case, we carried folks from the village with us. Paulino's baby was sick, and he and his wife wanted a ride to the small clinic in town. We pulled up to the unadorned cement building and let the family out. John

accompanied them inside to make sure they were received well and given attention. He came back with a shocking announcement

Two children from our community, ages 1 and 2, had died at the clinic. We'd been asked to transport their bodies back to the village. One had died just that morning. The other, however, had died on Monday, and this was Wednesday. My barely-settled stomach did another flip-flop.

The simple pleasure of choosing our groceries from the limited selection at one of the small food stores was eclipsed by my concern over the state of the body longest deceased.

I numbly went through the motions of selecting potatoes, onions, cabbage, and apples—foods that would keep for weeks without refrigeration. I also scanned the bloody slabs of meat behind the glass of the butcher's case and chose a kilo of ground beef. I added some canned fruits and vegetables, cheese cut to order from a massive block, tortillas, dry milk, cooking oil, and pinto beans. At the very end I picked out some melons and tomatoes, delicacies we would consume within the first few days of returning home.

The rest of the day passed in a blur. John had to track down a man with whom he had business. The kids picked out their trinkets and candies at *Novedades Ady*; we ate quesadillas and tacos and drank soda pop straight from cold glass bottles at Lupita's café.

At last it was time to pick up the bodies and head home. John drove slowly to the clinic and around to the back door. Clinic personnel helped load the remains of the children into the back of our Ram Charger. The one that had died two and a half days earlier was wrapped in a cloth and placed in a crude wood coffin. The one that had died that morning was also wrapped in a cloth, but was placed in a cardboard box. Both went in on top of our cargo of groceries and other supplies.

Paulino and his family were not returning with us, so our three kids had the backseat to themselves. But even though the trip home should have been more comfortable, I found that the two silent passengers stretched out behind the backseat screamed wordlessly for my attention. I worried about the condition of the one that had died earlier—would there be odor, could there be some kind of contamination? I recoiled at the reality of the other child having been tucked into a cardboard box. Every cell in my body objected; no cardboard box is sacred enough to transport a human body. And I felt an inconsolable agony that each child had died alone, with no parent keeping loving vigil by his side, and would show up unannounced and lifeless on his family's doorstep.

We passed the long trip without incident, and delivered the bodies to several nuns living in the valley who knew the families. I, however, continued to turn the experience over and over in my mind, seeking, as always, to make sense of things.

In the end I reconciled with the fact that life is filled, just as that difficult day was, with experiences that blindside us. Sometimes we must share small spaces with people who make us uncomfortable, rubbing shoulders with those very different from us, being acutely aware of their—and our—flawed humanity. Sometimes we get close enough to death to touch and smell it, having to look it straight in the eye, recognizing it is no respecter of persons. And sometimes we see our most holy dreams packed casually into a cardboard box and lowered into a deep, dark hole. In those moments the very foundations of earth seem to shake, and everything that matters begins to sway and totter. And then what? Where do we go? What do we do?

There is only one thing to do when the world makes no sense. Run to the One who has revealed Himself in His generous word. And reconcile with the fact that, while there is often clarity in life, there is also always mystery. Some things we can know plainly; others are hidden. Anchored in what we *know* is true—about this earth, about ourselves, about Him—we can more readily let rest the things we cannot understand. For He is the One who has said, "In this world you will have trouble. But take heart! I have overcome the world."

We find solace and safety and sense in Him and Him alone.

......

"My flesh and my heart may fail, but God is the strength of my heart and my portion forever." Psalm 73:26

BEAUTY IN A BROWN PAPER BAG

Beauty is hard-won here.

A small but sturdy picket fence keeps the cows and goats from my front stoop and forms a niche where my nasturtiums flourish. And while I watered the flowers with old dishwater one morning, twelve-year-old Guadalupe, her toddler niece tied to her back with a bright orange shawl, approached shyly and leaned against the low fence.

Assuming she was on her way somewhere, I smiled and asked where she was headed. She said simply, "Here."

I motioned toward the screen door. "Would you like to come in?"

Guadalupe self-consciously pushed open the gate and followed me into the kitchen. She set her niece on the cement floor and then sat quietly at the kitchen table while I made her a cup of hot chocolate. As she took her first sip of the frothy sweetness, I watched the corners of her mouth turn up in bashful approval, dark eyes peering at me over the top of the mug.

"I was going to go to *your* house today," I said.

Her eyes grew slightly wider, and she set the mug down on the table. She looked at me with great seriousness but said nothing. Guadalupe was not what anyone would call pretty. Her cheeks were wind-chapped and her features plain, but an openness and sincerity shone from her deep brown eyes.

"Andrea needs a new skirt," I said. "Would you like to make it?"

"Sí!" She said the word quietly but emphatically, nodding at the same time.

I brought out the fabric and called six-year-old Andrea into the kitchen. We measured her waist with a thin strip of fabric we tore from the larger piece and marked with a safety pin. Guadalupe repeated this process with another strip of fabric and measured from Andrea's waist to just below her knees for the skirt's length.

Tarahumara skirts are very full, made of multitudes of tiny pleats sewn by hand, and are embellished with a saw-tooth edge of contrasting fabric near the bottom. As was customary, I paid Guadalupe with an equal amount of the same fabric.

"How beautiful," she whispered, fingering the lavender floral print.

Then I packaged it all—her fabric, Andrea's fabric, some bright purple for the edging of both skirts, and a spool of purple thread—in a paper bag and placed it on the kitchen table next to her.

Guadalupe downed the hot chocolate, settled her stocky niece once more on her back, and left with the package clutched close to her heart. Two times she turned to look back at me before she went out the gate; she said nothing, but her face was radiant. I watched from the door as she hurried down the hill toward home, her faded skirt bouncing as she skipped along the worn path and then broke into a run. Several times she slowed to hoist the heavy toddler farther up her back.

Guadalupe lives in a hand-me-down world, where utility and purpose are wrung from every possession until nothing is left. New is not normal. Beauty is for someone else.

But that day, in triumph over her worn and common world, she carried that brown paper bag as if it contained all the colors of the rainbow. And in a way I believe it did—it bulged with shimmering hues of dignity and grace, value and longing. Guadalupe was so transfigured I could never again see her as plain.

To me, it had seemed a simple gift. To her, untold beauty was tucked inside that brown paper bag.

......

"He has made everything beautiful in its own time."
Ecclesiastes 3:11

OLD JAKE

I had come to a difficult peace over the plight of Tarahumara dogs and, out of self-protection, kept them confined to the periphery of my life. That is until Old Jake defied the laws of decency and plopped himself down at my feet.

Dogs abound in Tarahumara villages, but few are wanted, and even those kept by families are often malnourished, bony and hungry-eyed, surviving on the scant tortillas tossed in their direction.

One morning I stepped out onto our back porch, startled to see a large, mangy dog skulking in the nearby bushes. I stopped, expecting him to show aggression. He stood motionless, his haunted eyes flicking in my direction. When he sensed no threat from me, he hobbled to the edge of the small concrete porch, stepped up onto it, and collapsed. Large patches of his wiry grey-and-white hair had fallen out, leaving exposed flesh covered with scabs. Bones protruded everywhere on his body—his ribs could be counted, his hips jutted at sharp angles, and his legs were nothing more than knobby sticks. He was the most pathetic creature I had ever seen.

My heart lurched. I knew Tarahumara dogs simply did not enjoy the privileged status of American dogs, and to treat them in such manner would fly in the face of Tarahumara values. Yet something in the demeanor of this dog tore at me. He had surrendered, resigning himself to his impending death.

As I stared at the pitiful dog all the illness, ugliness, and death I had seen in the village during the past months reared up like a tidal wave. I could feel the surge of hopelessness wash over me; but instead of succumbing, I became angry.

In defiance of all the odds against everyone's life in that place, I decided to name the ragtag animal huddled near my door, to dignify him, to carve out a niche of significance for him in an uncaring world. His name would be Jake. Old Jake. Then I walked into the house, got some leftover bread, and fed Jake a small meal.

At noon I fed him again, a slightly larger portion, and at supper I repeated the process, this time sharing rice and beans. In three weeks we would be taking a trip back to the States, so I knew feeding Jake was at best a stopgap measure. But I couldn't help myself. Old Jake got three clandestine meals a day, and his crooked tail thumped on the cement each time I appeared, as if he could not believe his good fortune.

Jake's aged, broken-down body was beyond repair, and in spite of my care he never showed any signs of improvement. He wandered away from the porch various times during the day, and I wondered each time if he had gone off to die. He always came back, though, until it seemed he was determined to breathe his last on my doorstep.

My compulsion to feed Old Jake was driven by my utter helplessness to alter the difficult course of life lived by the Tarahumara. The things John and I did to effect change in the community seemed so minute, so inconsequential, in the face of overwhelming needs. I felt like a David standing before the Goliath of infant mortality, poor nutrition and dirty water, lack of education, alcoholism, and domestic violence. I was completely dwarfed and, to be honest, tempted at times to throw down my sling and run. The act of caring for a dying dog was something tangible, something do-able, and became inexplicably essential, as if that act could change the course of human history.

It didn't, of course. At the end of three weeks, Old Jake looked no better than the day of his arrival. We bid him a gentle good-bye and headed for the border. He was gone when we returned, and neighbors informed us of his death.

Through this and other experiences, God drove me to examine my response to the overwhelming odds against life and beauty that exist in many parts of this world. I wrestled with the danger (and still do) of becoming paralyzed by darkness and evil, forgetting to do even a small *something* to fight it.

When we stand puny today against the giants of homelessness, sex-trafficking, famine, and HIV/AIDS we need to boldly proclaim as David did to Goliath, "I come against you in the name of the Lord Almighty…whom you have defied." We cannot lose hope in the collective impact of all our small *somethings*. And we must pick up the seemingly inadequate stones of love, and grace, and action that lie within our reach and fling them by faith against the great hurts of this world.

……

"Do not be overcome by evil, but overcome evil with good."
Romans 12:21

SAMUEL'S QUESTION

Our neighbor Samuel showed up at the door one day to see my husband, urgency evident in his expression and stance.

"I have a question," he said to John. "How can I love the Lord with all my heart, with all my mind, with all my soul and with all my strength, and go out and get firewood at the same time?"

His question stirred a smile within me. It reflected such a child-like, literal perspective. It appeared somehow simplistic and small. But as the days wore on the question dogged me, and the more I turned it over in my mind, the more I wondered why I myself had never tripped and stumbled over those very words of Jesus.

For in its innocence, Samuel's question actually frames one of the larger struggles of my life.

How *do* I live my life as an inhabitant of another Kingdom, all the while held firmly to this planet not only by the laws of gravity, but also those of dirty floors and diminishing stacks of firewood?

How do I love the Lord with everything I am and have an ounce of anything left for any other task? Or, conversely, how do I care for the children, go to my job, weed the garden, take the car to the mechanic and still engage with all my heart, mind, soul, and strength in loving my great God?

You see, I'm a compartmentalist. I prefer tidy boxes in which to file all of life's activities. I like to think I can somehow finish all the daily mundane and then move on, undistracted, to what is holy. When I live like that I have missed the boat. Not only that, but the boat has left and I'm not even aware it existed.

Life is not an either/or proposition. It can never be singularly physical or spiritual. It cannot be neatly parceled into sacred and common. Rather, life is one ungainly heap of everything it means to be human— burden and blessing, work and worship, sorrow and satisfaction.

Drawing tidy lines in the sand of life leads not only to a false sense of how to live my days, but also a failure to recognize the beauty of the whole. It drives me to view the many parts of my existence as contradictory, incompatible. It abandons me to feelings of fragmentation, when in reality I am offered wholeness, a mysterious blending of the Laws of the Universe and the inexplicable Offerings of Heaven. That is where I am meant to live. Smack dab in the middle of flesh and blood and spirit and longing. Right at the interface of tangible and intangible.

Many define sacrament as a visible sign of an inward grace. There, I believe, lies our invitation. We are beckoned into sacramental living, into the broad view of life's holiness, into an integrated expression of our life of work and our love of God. The vegetable garden is, in reality, a place of worship; planting, weeding, watering, and harvesting are acts of great faith and purpose that honor God. Washing clothes, preparing food, changing a tire, and painting the house are not what we get out of the way in order to later know and worship God, but instead are to be mindfully woven into our love of and life in Him. The way we do each task, greet each person, submit to each interruption is to be a visible sign of an inward grace, an embracing of the sacredness of the necessary, an affirmation that God is everywhere present, inviting us always to find ourselves in Him.

Samuel nailed it. Though he possessed only a grade-school education, his theological and philosophical understanding far outstripped mine. Somehow he intuitively grasped the mystery that defines our lives in this world, and he peeled back the layers of this enigma so I could wonder at it too.

......

"For in him we live and move and have our being."
Acts 17:28

OF COWS AND CLOTHES

In no time laundry day loomed dreadful on the horizon of each week. I quickly began scheming ways to clean our clothes without lugging them to the *arroyo* and washing them beside the stream on a rock.

Since we hauled water in buckets from a hand pump an eighth mile from our house, I made every drop count. Water was used and then used again. After washing and rinsing dishes, the wash water went outside to keep my meager flowers alive. The rinse water was poured into the wash basin to be used for cleaning the next meal's dishes.

Similarly, I began to recycle bath water. After our children's weekly baths, taken one after the other in the same water in a small galvanized tub, I added laundry detergent to the leftover water and soaked the dirtiest of our blue jeans, then later scrubbed them clean in the luxury of my own small kitchen.

For white underwear and socks, I resorted to using clean water, and filled a 5-gallon bucket from the hand pump or adjacent spring. To this I added detergent and all the unmentionables and then placed the bucket on the back porch to soak overnight. I harbored no aspirations of having the "whitest whites"; I only cared to get out the majority of the ground-in dirt and dust. After letting the clothes soak overnight, I used a plunger to agitate them in the bucket, then rinsed them and clipped them to a clothesline to dry.

One late fall morning after the corn had been harvested and the animals again roamed freely in the valley, I stepped onto the back porch en route to the outhouse. I was only half-heartedly embracing the new day. In my typical overly-responsible way I had been trying to be everything to everybody. I'd been cheerfully welcoming (outwardly, at least) all the Tarahumara visitors who appeared at my door, while trying to homeschool our kids, brainstorm creative ways to serve beans and tortillas again, and try to keep up with everything else essential to daily life. I somehow believed the well-being of my family in this unusual place depended on me and me alone. I was worn out and disillusioned.

To my dismay, I discovered the underwear bucket I'd left on the porch the night before had been tipped over, the water spilled completely out. Underwear and socks were scattered everywhere in the dirt, and twenty feet away stood an unfamiliar cow chewing contentedly on something white. I lunged at the cow and wrestled the underwear from her unyielding mouth, then slapped her on the behind and chased her away. As I surveyed the scene I noticed that most, if not all, of the muddy articles scattered in a semicircle around the porch had sizeable holes chewed in them. The cow had apparently tasted each before settling on her favorite.

I was instantly flooded with anger, then fear. What if a pair of four-year-old Luke's Superman underwear became lodged in one of the several stomachs of the cow? What if the prized animal died from this obstruction and while it was being slaughtered, the offending item was discovered? Who else besides us in this whole remote valley owned Superman underwear?

I grabbed the bucket and began gathering the remnants of our now-filthy laundry, further irritated as the cow kept sneaking up behind me in an attempt to snatch another sock or piece of underwear. As if she'd not yet made a sufficient spectacle of me.

I hit a low spot that day. I felt like the community clown and kept looking over my shoulder to see if any Tarahumara neighbors were enjoying a laugh at my expense. To my knowledge no one else was privy to the ridiculous scene. The embarrassing secret was mine alone. And my family's too, of course, since they had to wear holey underwear and socks until we could make the three-hour drive to town and buy more.

After washing the last of the muddy cow saliva from the salvaged bucket of laundry, I regrouped with a cup of tea. As I poured out my frustration and anxieties to God my perspective slowly returned. I was even able to laugh at myself for letting a cow get the best of me. I began to see how a small setback became almost insurmountable simply because I was exhausted, lonely, and setting unrealistic expectations for myself.

God employed the services of a cow to show me that neediness comes in all shapes and sizes, many of which are a perfect fit for me. In assuming responsibility to make everything right for everyone around me, I was living as if it's all about me and was stealing from God's goodness. I needed to let God be God. And I needed to let me be me—weak, weary, and needy though I was.

In the end everything worked out. I never heard of anyone's cow dying. No one showed up at my house angrily waving a pair of shredded Superman underwear. And I got to take a much-needed deep breath and slowly let it out.

......

"Come to me, all you who are weary and burdened,
and I will give you rest." Matthew 11:28

ALL THINGS NEW

One night the weather shifted, and we awoke to heavy frost and wispy fog covering the valley. In spite of the freezing temperatures outside, the wood stove in our small kitchen radiated warmth and kept us comfortable. I wondered about other families scattered throughout the valley, knowing many slept on dirt floors in drafty cabins.

The simple log house we were renting from a young Tarahumara couple had required some renovations. So that we could stand up in it, John had dug the dirt floor down another foot, then poured a cement floor. On this morning, dirt rained into the kitchen from the mud-packed ceiling as John and Modesto hammered new hand-split pine shingles onto the roof. Later, John put a toilet seat in our new outhouse. We felt quite indulged, even if the little building didn't yet have a roof or door.

That afternoon, a radiant Indian summer day, an important footrace began in our valley. Two teams, each consisting of two men, were slated to run a difficult course over mountain paths while kicking a hand-carved wood ball the size of a baseball. The entire race would last nearly 24 hours. Each of the runners wore handmade sandals, the soles of which had been cut from old tires and were held to their feet with leather thongs. One of the runners had come by our house earlier in the day asking if we had tape he could use to wrap his bare toes. He left with duct tape protecting all ten toes from the ravages of the wooden ball.

At 8:00 p.m. we caught our first glimpse of the race. Far down in the pitch-black valley, a host of twinkling lights appeared, snaking their way toward us. We stood transfixed in the velvet darkness outside our house, listening to the muffled voices and occasional shouts, watching as the lights grew larger and the teams eventually ran up the path directly toward us. Alongside each team ran a group of helpers with crude torches held high, lighting the way for the runners. As the racers passed our house we could see the torches consisted of tin cans, sliced vertically and spread apart like Chinese lanterns. Inside each a pitchy substance burned brightly, and the cans hung from the

ends of sticks, fishing-pole style. Some members of each support team carried small pails of water mixed with *covisi*, finely ground popped corn, a favorite Tarahumara drink that would nourish and energize the runners.

All five of us stood spellbound as the racers and their friends swept past our house. And then they disappeared into the night again while we lingered, listening until the low, urgent rhythm of their voices and the thudding of their feet faded into the blackness.

We stood still and silent, processing the image, until Kristen summed it up. "That was better than watching the Olympics!" she said.

I agreed. Better, yet decidedly stranger. I felt as if I was in another world, but then that was exactly where I was.

It was a world where all things were new, and strange, and in many ways wonderful. But it was also a world, like the one I'd left, that grappled daily with loss, discord, violence, isolation, and death. A world that writhed in anguish, longing to birth within itself only what is beautiful and good but finding always, as is true the world over, that such a hope is impossible to attain.

The stunning God-image stamped on each person and culture has been heart-wrenchingly twisted, marred, and defiled by sin, and no amount of human effort can ever achieve the newness we so desperately long for.

Our only hope—and an outrageous one at that—is an invitation to exchange the old for the new, to enter into an astonishing new covenant, to be endowed with new life, to be dignified with a new name, and to one day experience the new heavens and the new earth.

There is *only One* who makes such a bold offer, who possesses such transformative power, and who can make good on such astounding promises.

That One is Jesus, the Lamb who sits upon the throne, the One who alone has authority to proclaim, "I am making everything new!"

......

"And I heard a loud voice from the throne saying, 'Look! God's dwelling place is now among the people, and he will dwell with them. They will be his people, and God himself will be with them and be their God. He will wipe every tear from their eyes. There will be no more death or mourning or crying or pain, for the old order of things has passed away.' He who was seated on the throne said, 'I am making everything new!'" Revelation 21:3-5

WHAT ABOUT CHRISTMAS?

My family cherishes its own unique Christmas traditions, just as yours does. Included in our list of specialties is a Finnish delicacy we make only this time of year—pinwheel-shaped tarts of handmade, buttery puff pastry with a sweet filling of cooked prunes. After the Christmas Eve candlelight service, we always hurry home to enjoy, among other things, steaming hot French-Canadian pork pie. Our tree sparkles with small white lights which form the backdrop for an eclectic mix of hand-picked ornaments, each with a story, no two alike. Decorating the tree is a retelling of our family history. As each tissue-wrapped ornament is removed from its box and placed on a branch, people and stories are recalled with smiles and laughter or an occasional tear of remembrance. Nativities representing various ethnicities are scattered throughout the house, baby Jesus depicted in each as one of their own, with distinct skin and hair color, eye shape, and native clothing.

Our traditions are not lavish; in fact, many are quite simple. But over the years they have come to define us and what Christmas means to our family. They root us in the much bigger picture of Christ's birth and provide a continuity that has allowed us to carve out a sacred sameness from year to year in a world that is constantly changing.

Not so our first year among the Tarahumara.

Our world was in a state of dramatic change that year. We were two months into our new lives in a Tarahumara Indian village. December was cold, but brown—a far cry from the snowy beauty that had characterized most of my previous

Christmases. It had taken every ounce of my physical and emotional energy to move our family of five to this primitive setting, and I had failed to think ahead to Christmas. In early December I felt twinges of panic and began to ask myself, "What about Christmas?" The five of us bounced three hours over dirt roads one day to the nearest town, a small rough-and-tumble conglomeration of houses and simple stores, and John and I secretly bought little gifts for the children—small stuffed animals, pens, notebooks, and Mexican candy.

Back in the village, we dug up a 2-foot evergreen tree, planted it in a galvanized pail, and gave it a place of honor on our small kitchen table. The kids strung it with handmade paper chains and other things they crafted. There were no twinkling white lights. We didn't even have electricity. Without butter, puff pastry was out of the question, and I didn't even let my mind wander to thoughts of pork pie. While I fretted over the absence of our usual traditions and busied myself trying to create some sense of festivity for my family, the kids threw themselves into the season with abandon. They made gifts for the family with whatever was at hand—clothes for a stuffed bear from fabric scraps, a book of coupons good for extra chores, a first-aid kit made from a tin can filled with Band-Aids and Q-Tips. Kristen even made a corncob nativity scene.

We found a discarded 15-inch-diameter wooden wheel and made an advent wreath from it. When we lit the first candle, I got a lump in my throat to see the faces of all three children filled with anticipation, eyes aglow. At this point they had no regrets about what our new home did not have to offer. Instead they embraced the novelty and adventure.

As Christmas approached, the small group of Tarahumara Christians announced they would have a Christmas Eve service in the late afternoon. We walked three-quarters of a mile in a bitter wind to the unheated log church building, which offered meager respite from the cold. We sang songs with strange melodies in a language I barely knew. We huddled in winter jackets on low plank benches and listened to people speak, clueless as to what was being said. There was no candlelight, no holiday finery, no smell of evergreen, no strains of "O Holy Night." The service ended and we stood around visiting with people to the best of our ability.

By the time we stepped outside the sun was going down and someone had a fire blazing on the rocky outcropping upon which the church sat. From somewhere an enormous skillet appeared, huge scoops of pig fat were added to it, and women began slicing potatoes into the sizzling lard. Coffee was boiled in a big pot then strained into a 5-gallon plastic bucket that had a large Shell Oil logo on its side.

When the bucket was full of steaming black coffee and the potatoes were tender, the women produced baskets of thick blue corn tortillas brought from home. Coffee was ladled into chipped enamel mugs and served with sugar. Potatoes were heaped on tortillas and eaten with fingers from worn plastic plates.

I was ravenous, and as we huddled around the fire savoring the simple food, I glanced from face to face illumined in the golden flames. It hit me hard that it was to a ragtag bunch such as ours that angels appeared one cold Bethlehem night, to simple souls likely gathered around a fire, to people who had more questions than answers. Absent any twinkling lights, any dainty tarts, any festive wrapping paper, the greatest gift had been given and received that faraway night.

The fire in front of me crackled, a child whined, dogs tussled, and the conversation slowly hushed while weary faces grew pensive. As I shivered against the cold night, I realized that the poverty, humility, and simplicity surrounding me were what the first Christmas, the real Christmas, was all about, and that all of us come always as paupers to the manger.

The lavishness of Divine provision in the face of our stark impoverishment is what makes the Night of nights so astonishing.

Yes indeed...what *about* Christmas?

All the world over, each of us stands alone under a starry sky, empty-handed beggars looking up, invited into the Song of the Ages. It's up to us whether or not we listen.

That night I heard it. Loud and clear. The unmistakable strains of a hallowed announcement to a worn-out world. And it took my breath away.

......

> "And there were shepherds living out in the fields nearby, keeping watch over their flocks at night. An angel of the Lord appeared to them and the glory of the Lord shone around them, and they were terrified. But the angel said to them, 'Do not be afraid. I bring you good news of great joy that will be for all the people. Today in the town of David a Savior has been born to you; he is Christ the Lord.'"
> Luke 2:8-11

CHICKEN SOUP

Berta showed up at my door one January day, saying her dad was sick and she wanted to make him a pot of chicken soup from a freshly-butchered hen. She wondered if she could cook it over my little two-burner gas camp stove because gas cooks faster than a wood fire does. Of course I said yes, but I smiled inwardly at her misconception. Because it was winter, a fire blazed all day in her family's *calenton*, or barrel stove, providing instant access to high heat cooking.

In the months I'd lived in the village I had, surprisingly, come to prefer cooking over my wood stove, using the gas option only on sweltering days when I didn't want to heat the kitchen. Although only three feet wide by two feet deep, my wood stove offered infinite variations in temperature. I quickly learned to slide my pot or cast-iron skillet an inch or two one way or the other, slightly closer or farther from the firebox below, in order to intensify the cooking or reduce it to a slow simmer.

I could also open the oven door, wave my hand through its interior, and determine if it had reached the proper temperature to bake the loaves rising in pans on the kitchen table, as if I were an accomplished backwoods chef overseeing a batch of artisan bread. When adding a stick of firewood, I knew exactly what type and size to insert in order to bump the oven temperature up a few degrees or maintain a slow, steady heat.

In spite of the fact that Berta's barrel stove was not as sophisticated as even my simple wood stove, its boiling power was equal. And I knew even my gas stove would not cook a pot of chicken soup any faster than her red-hot *calenton* would. Her confidence in the ability of my gas stove to produce results her barrel stove was incapable of was completely misplaced.

I am just like Berta, attributing power to things in my life that in reality have no control over the outcome.

I am a master at circumstantial justification. And I find this convoluted process of self-deception always begins with two simple words—*if only*. Maybe you've tinkered with such self-deception, too:

If only I had a nicer, bigger, or cleaner house I would invite people over.

If only I could afford a gym membership, a treadmill, or a new bicycle I would be in better shape.

If only I had an extra hour every day I would spend time with God.

If only I had access to a gourmet kitchen, expensive ingredients, and could produce food-blog results, I would eat healthier.

The excuses are varied and endless, but the result is always the same—the status quo. I've found that disempowering these foolish notions and making healthy progress always boils down to three steps:

The honest step (asking tough questions)—how do I really spend my time, where does my money actually go, what priorities do my choices truly reveal?

The bold step (taking a new course of action)—Am I willing to get up a half hour earlier than the rest of the household, will I push away from activities that ultimately undermine my productivity, will I set goals and start taking small steps toward them?

The scary step (inviting someone in)—do I dare seek out a friend who will hold my feet to the fire, ask the hard questions, not be thrown off by smokescreen answers?

Berta believed that something just beyond her reach was surely superior to the resources at hand—a deadly deception we are all tempted to embrace. If each of us was only willing to work with the barrel stove we already have, untold pots of chicken soup could be produced, ultimately nourishing the souls of many.

......

"He who is faithful in a very little thing
is faithful also in much..." Luke 16:10 (NASB)

SOLITARY LABOR

Childbirth is intertwined with old wives' tales the world over, and the Tarahumara have their own unique perspectives on it. My neighbor Rosa informed me that many of the women give birth at home alone because if others are present the baby will be embarrassed and delay being born, thus prolonging labor. I wondered if it wasn't the mother who was embarrassed; although once immersed in labor, it's a rare woman who would try to prolong the experience because of any perceived impropriety.

On another occasion, while watching Martina fire her handmade clay pots in an open flame, I mentioned having recently seen Elena, obviously pregnant, also making pots. Martina clucked disapprovingly and told me a pregnant woman should never make pots because it causes the baby to become very large.

By far the most remarkable event, however, occurred when petite young Esperanza slipped out of her house in the middle of a cold night, trekked up the mountainside in labor, and gave birth all by herself on the bare ground. It was her first child, and she had the daring and presence of mind to deliver that baby boy in the dark, all alone, far from assistance of any kind. Her husband told us how surprised he was to wake up the next morning as she walked through the door with a baby in her arms.

I have wrestled many times with Esperanza's story, horrified by the possibility of different outcomes. What if the baby was breach and could not be born? Or what if Esperanza had hemorrhaged to death, leaving the newborn unprotected on the rocky hillside? Aside from avoiding life and death scenarios, didn't she wish for someone to tell her: "Don't worry, this is normal" or "You're getting close; it will soon be over"? To this day I marvel at her misplaced confidence, her audacity.

Cultural customs and beliefs aside, giving birth is a natural process that, while progressing most often without complication, is made better and safer by the loving support of others.

To how many things have I given birth in seclusion over the years, a solitary laborer in a lonely landscape? How many times have I struggled to complete a task, refusing to ask for help whether out of embarrassment or stubbornness or a misguided sense of responsibility? How many times have I compromised the viability of something important because I wouldn't include others, wanting to show up in the end with the "baby" in my—

and only my—arms? How many times did I miss the joy of collaboration because honestly, laboring together is supremely messy?

I know the answer. Far too many times.

To my shame, I've often taken what seemed the easier route of just doing it myself when in fact it was the risky choice, the lonely one, the less supported one.

Too often I've been guilty of choosing a solitary rocky mountainside over the solidarity and strength of others.

What audacity. What misplaced confidence. What immeasurable loss.

......

"Two are better than one, because they have a good return for their work: If one falls down, his friend can help him up. But pity the man who falls and has no one to help him up!" Ecclesiastes 4:9-10

SUCH AS THESE

I used to love artistic renditions of Jesus with little children on His lap. Now I resent them.

The children in these pictures always have neatly combed hair and scrubbed faces and wear spotless, unwrinkled clothes. They're sparkling-eyed pictures of health. And when they climb onto Jesus' white-robed lap they don't get even a speck of dirt on Him.

This doesn't ring true in my world today, much less in the rural, labor-intensive world where Jesus walked. And I know such visions of cleanliness and order are impossible to achieve in the earthy world of the Tarahumara.

Tarahumara homes are small and families are large. Most live with dirt floors, work hard to make corn and beans and potatoes grow from the resistant earth, haul their water in buckets, and wash their clothes by hand. And as I look into the faces of their children, with tear streaks tracing paths along dusty cheeks, with dirty noses and tangled hair, I think *these* are the children Jesus embraced, *these* are the types He touched and hugged—not the clean, presentable children of the wishful artwork I used to enjoy.

Giving a beautiful glimpse into the heart of Jesus, His friend Mark tells us that "people were bringing little children to Jesus to have him touch them, but the disciples rebuked them." Indignant, Jesus overruled, declaring that the Kingdom of God belongs to such as these. "And he took the children in his arms, put his hands on them and blessed them."

He may have wrapped His arms around a sickly child. He may have welcomed an impoverished one with ragged, dirty clothing. He may have laid His hands on lice-infested heads. He embraced the children in spite of, or perhaps because of, their unpretentious approach, their coming just as they were—plain and ordinary in the broad light of day.

Yes, the Kingdom of God belongs to such as these, to the ones who accept Christ with an uncomplicated, childlike faith. But it also belongs to those who, like children, don't wait to clean up before coming to Jesus. To those who don't have it all figured out before running to Him. It belongs to those who climb dead broke, tarnished and empty, without inhibition, onto the Savior's lap.

We all have dirty noses. Our heads crawl at times with things that bring us shame. The faces we think we've polished bear unmistakable tear streaks. We stand bedraggled with pockets inside out and empty, in more ways than one.

Powerless to make ourselves presentable, what do we do? We abandon the pretense and we go. Straight to Jesus. Like a child, bashful or bold, inching or scrambling.

He stands, arms wide, waiting to embrace our dirt, with an offer to wrap our sin-soiled hearts in His cleanness.

And He will take us in His arms, He will put His hands on us, and He will bless us.

......

"Jesus said, 'Let the little children come to me, and do not hinder them, for the kingdom of heaven belongs to such as these.'"
Matthew 19:14

CASI MIRA

A young blind woman was our neighbor during our early weeks in the village while we lived with co-workers until finding a place of our own. Whenever she ventured from home, her young daughter led her slowly along the uneven trails. They went hand in hand, the daughter slightly out front choosing the way, the mother following cautiously, her baby boy secured snugly to her back with a shawl. The woman was introduced to me as Casi Mira, the two words meaning in Spanish "almost sees." It seemed an appropriate name, even if an unkind declaration of her condition.

Casi Mira became a regular visitor at the house where we were staying. A typical Tarahumara, she did not knock at the door, but stood on the porch with her children until I heard them. I would invite her in and give her a cup of coffee and, if I had one, a tortilla. Her daughter and baby played on the floor at her feet while she sat quietly for long periods of time despite my attempts at conversation. She was not afflicted with my American compulsion to fill the emptiness around us with words.

Inevitably, when a suitable length of time had passed according to her standards, she would reveal the purpose for her visit. She had no thread; did I have a spool she could have? Or, she needed a sewing needle; could I give her one? Or, she was out of sugar; could I spare a bit? And as she inquired, she reached under the layers of shawl wrapped around her and produced a small stack of corn tortillas she had made. As I traded with her, tortillas for some simple commodity, I was moved by the sense of dignity that prevented her from simply asking me to give her things, as other neighbors had.

We never ate Casi Mira's tortillas; they came wrapped in a piece of dirty cloth and were likely made with nearby contaminated stream water. Yet each time I received them with gratitude. To have declined them for any reason would have dishonored her.

As months passed I discovered that, oddly, Casi Mira was not an unusual name for Tarahumara women. Having assumed my neighbor Casi Mira had been given the name Almost Sees to reflect her near-blindness, I began to ask others about her story. Was she born blind? When did her parents discover her lack of sight? I learned she was not born blind, that she had enjoyed normal sight until early adulthood when she suddenly lost her vision.

I was stunned. When given to her, the name had no connection with lack of eyesight. How strange, I thought. An innocent name came to define her, as if a self-fulfilling prophecy.

Despite my inability to understand the situation, Casi Mira became a banner waving over my days. Every time I saw her, one irrefutable truth was proclaimed. Words matter.

Words matter. With my words I can affirm what is beautiful, nurture goodness in a child, give strength to the struggling, or be the believing voice that propels someone to great achievement. My words can also unravel confidence, chip away at dignity, or foster in someone an image of flat nothingness that will become a self-fulfilling indictment.

It's both a terrifying and motivating truth that my words have the power to define others. I am crushed when I find myself speaking words that wound and tear. I am humbled and ever-so-grateful when my words nurture and heal. Clearly, in my desire to be one who speaks words of life, I desperately need Jesus, the One who is the good and holy Word made flesh.

Years later I discovered the name I was hearing as two words, Casi Mira, was actually one word, Casimira, and had an entirely different meaning altogether, nothing to do with sight. God used my linguistic misunderstanding to good ends, however. The simple, uneducated woman who walked those mountain trails in the shadows of blindness shed light into my life without ever knowing it. Casimira actually opened *my* eyes and helped me ponder the power of my words.

......

"The tongue has the power of life and death..." Proverbs 18:21

MICE IN THE MIDDLE OF THE NIGHT

5:00 a.m. March 1—I've been up for a half hour now, having been roused from sleep by sharp mouse claws scampering across my cheek. The mouse is now trapped, struggling, inside the cover of the comforter waiting for John to get up and dispose of it. Meanwhile, I have started a crackling fire in the kitchen stove and have lit several candles by which to read and write.

The children's poem *I Think Mice are Rather Nice* comes to mind. At the moment I do not think they are very nice at all. Field mice are fine but this mouse, in running across my face, has violated all the universal rules of conduct that exist between humans and rodents. As I think about it, many rules of conduct have been violated by many creatures over the past months. Between mice, lizards, vinegaroons, and black widows I've honestly begun to think we live in a wild animal house.

Sometimes I wonder how I can stand to live like this. How much more do I have to give? Usually I offer up my inconveniences as a sacrifice to God, but my reading this morning has me wondering about my heart.

God pulls the rug out from under some people's pious preconceptions when, in Psalm 50, He says He doesn't need the animals sacrificed as Old Testament offerings. "I have no need of a bull from your stall or of goats from your pens, for every animal of the forest is mine, and the cattle on a thousand hills." But twice in the same psalm He speaks of *thank offerings*, as if urging us deeper so that we might get an accurate picture of our elusive hearts. "Sacrifice thank offerings to God. . ." and "He who sacrifices thank offerings honors me . . ."

When the sacrifice of my life lived here (or anywhere) becomes one of pure obligation, given out of a sense of duty rather than offered freely out of a sense of joy and thanksgiving, I am like those misdirected Old Testament worshipers whose sacrifice became constrained and stingy. For this is the very attitude that reduced worship—what was intended to be a relationship-building act—into a rote activity of routine sacrifice that held little significance for God or man.

How easily I wander into that murky terrain between a genuinely thankful heart willing to joyfully give and one that merely goes through the motions.

The fact that I've had eyes mostly for the negative lately—that my focus has been on what's wrong, and that I've been quick to see what's not happening—reveals my deep need to cultivate the practice of thanksgiving.

God is not honored by my hollow sacrifice. Instead, He invites me to break dead cycles of outward compliance and waken my heart to life-giving thankfulness.

So, I'm still not a fan of mice that push boundaries, but in the end it was a pretty good wake up call.

......

"Through Jesus, therefore, let us continually offer to God a sacrifice of praise…" Hebrews 13:15

A GLAD WELCOME

One early spring day, Andrea, Luke, and I ventured to the far end of the valley where the forest begins to encroach on fields and sparse houses. We wanted to find Lupita's house and see her new baby. I carried a small gift—a homemade flannel blanket, an infant shirt, and knitted baby booties—one of several layettes that had been given me to share with new mothers.

After much meandering we found her house. She and a little girl of four or five were sitting outside on a pile of what I presumed were cast-off clothes. It was one of the first warm days of the season and all of our winter-weary bodies drank up the sunshine with an unquenchable thirst.

I had always wondered about Lupita; her face bears the look of mild mental retardation, but I could not be sure. As far as I knew she spoke little Spanish, so we began our encounter with a significant handicap. I fumbled through my limited repertoire of Tarahumara words, inquiring about the baby, discovering it was a girl. Then I handed her the little gift. I pointed to the blanket and said *kimaca*—blanket in Tarahumara. For the shirt, I resorted to Spanish—*camisa*— then I picked up the delicate white booties and pointed to my feet and hers since the baby was nowhere to be seen.

Her face was impassive. I think there was a brief flicker of response in her eyes (or did I just hope so?), but there was no change in expression, no smile, no sense of glad reception of the little gift. She laid the small bundle of baby things on her lap and continued picking through the old clothes upon which she sat, finding small scraps and smoothing them with her fingers—perhaps bits of fabric she wished to reuse?

I stood awkwardly by. She did not motion for me to sit down, nor did she offer to let me see the baby. She made no attempts at conversation. I let my eyes roam over my surroundings. The yard was neat though barren, as was all the landscape this time of year.

Over the course of the next fifteen minutes I made small talk, commenting on all the firewood her husband had stacked nearby, asking if the young girl beside her was her daughter, and inquiring about who owned the house across the field. To all my questions Lupita gave a brief reply; some of her words I understood, some I did not. After further silence I decided it was time to leave. "Well, I'm going now, *Ma cu simi*," I said.

"You are going now," she said.

Was there a flicker of surprise that I was leaving so soon? Or was it relief? I lightly touched her hand in a parting handshake, and my children and I walked slowly away.

I was not discouraged by the encounter. It was essentially what I had expected. For a newcomer to any culture, the barriers to communication are enormous and the implications can be paralyzing if one thinks too long and hard about them.

I did, however, ponder the little bundle of delicate baby things, newly made, clean and pretty, that I had given Lupita. I wondered if she was even now unfolding them, fingering their softness, trying them on her baby. Was she glad for something new and lovely for her infant daughter? Those were things about which I could only speculate.

But one thing was certain. Into this dry brown world of barren fields and mud houses came a little life, new and fresh and hopeful for itself even if no one else was. I wanted that baby to know the touch of a soft shirt and to wiggle her tiny toes inside a velvety blanket. I longed for her to experience a glad welcome, extended through the wide-open arms of all around her. I willed for her the knowledge that, even in our obscurity, we are known and loved, and that we matter deeply to this big world and even more so to its purposeful Maker.

......

> "Whoever welcomes one of these little children in my name welcomes me; and whoever welcomes me does not welcome me but the one who sent me." Mark 9:37

A DILEMMA OF CHOICE

Leaving the village for any length of time involved an enormous amount of work. Knowing mice would inevitably multiply and become bold in our absence, I packed any food not in cans into large plastic bins. I wrapped extra bedding and any clothing we didn't take in layers of plastic to keep it clean. Our clothes for the trip, homeschooling materials, car-repair tools, and everything else needed during our absence was loaded into the car. And, of course, good-byes had to be said.

On one particular pre-trip day many Tarahumara stopped in to say good-bye. Each visit had to be honored with an acceptable amount of non-hurried chatting as we answered questions about where we were going, how many miles away it was, when we were coming back, and—a favorite request—could we bring some American fabric when we returned? As the number of visits mounted, I was glad I'd had the foresight to do the bulk of the packing earlier.

When at last I secured a few quiet moments, I crawled into bed, aching with fever and chills. Inez came by, and I heard John tell her I was sick in bed. When, after a while, he excused himself and stepped out the door, old Inez got up and shuffled around the corner to our bedroom. She stood there, inquiring genuinely about my well-being but also letting her eyes wander intentionally around the room, as if on a fact-finding mission. I knew she would have words to share about what the gringos' bedroom looked like. A good-hearted old woman I loved dearly, she also came bearing *covisi* (ground popped corn) which she hoped I might buy for our trip. I did.

We were up at 3 a.m. the next morning and on the road by 4:00, bouncing for hours over dirt roads, relieved when we came to pavement. The day was long, and as we traveled we ate the simple foods I had packed for the trip. In one rural Mexican town we passed a tiny restaurant of chipped turquoise stucco with a hand-lettered sign identifying it as "Burger the King." We chuckled and voted unanimously to save our growing appetites for American food that evening.

We crossed the border around dusk, and as always, I was a bit taken aback by the professional aloofness of the Border Patrol. Surely part of their job description should have included welcoming us home with a hug, a smile, and a free pass on all the technicalities of international law! At any rate, we were happy to be back in the good old USA.

We drove to a small southern Arizona town and stopped at a modest restaurant. Inside, we found ourselves blinking in the brightness of the artificial lighting, having just spent six months with only kerosene lamps and candles. After settling into a booth, we began reading the menu aloud, sharing excited conversation about foods we couldn't wait to eat again.

In the confusion, seven-year-old Andrea remained silent. When at last she spoke, she announced plainly that she wanted beans and tortillas. Nothing sounded good except beans and tortillas. We all stared at her. *Really?* In the village we ate beans and tortillas every day, sometimes twice a day. They were good, but here was a chance to eat *anything*...chicken and mashed potatoes, hamburgers, fresh green salad, pizza. The sky was the limit.

While I laugh sympathetically over Andrea's limited culinary vision, I also realize this is characteristic of how we often choose to live. We insist on eating peasant food when in reality Jesus has set a feast before us. We continue to subsist on what we've always known, all the while ignoring the One who offers what is exquisitely fulfilling. We consume things that can never satisfy and return to them again and again.

Hours that can never be recaptured are traded to earn material possessions that will never last. Stubbornness and pride claim our hearts, and we choose to believe mending broken relationships is just too costly. Activity becomes synonymous with meaningful productivity. Busyness eclipses relationship. Like sugar junkies we seek the quick fix of feel-good philosophies instead of slowing down and feeding ourselves on the whole, sometimes-hard-to-chew, life-giving Word of God.

Over and over again we refuse what truly nourishes and consume what leaves us hollow and empty.

As far as Andrea's dilemma was concerned, in the end we convinced her to try something different. And as far as my dilemma is concerned, I have learned to pray, "Lord, let me never be satisfied with the monotonous daily fare I'm inclined to choose, but give me an insatiable hunger for You and Your ways."

......

> "Why spend money on what is not bread, and your labor on what does not satisfy? Listen, listen to me, and eat what is good, and your soul will delight in the richest of fare." Isaiah 55:2

CONSPIRACY OF THE COMMON

I am the regular victim of attempted robbery. Without fail the world conspires daily to steal from me, to whisk away the beautiful from my presence, or at least blind me to beauty's reality and significance. Why? Because beauty is representative of all the glory and outrageous good that Jesus holds out to me.

In its mad rush the world shouts at me not to slow my frenzied pace, not to look, not to listen, not to ponder. In its deep brokenness it taunts me not to dare believe, not to hope, not to work for resurrection life.

The world tries without ceasing to convince me that everything is common and without value, when in reality I live in an expansive Kingdom of great worth and significance and beauty.

Life in the simplicity of the village was actually quite complicated. The routine of daily survival in an unfamiliar place often weighed heavily on me. What were easy tasks back home were laborious ordeals in my new environment— laundry, grocery shopping (3 hours away), cooking, and cleaning. Even simply communicating and navigating the uncharted waters of my neighbors' expectations added to my daily challenges.

When the dry winds of spring picked up force, I could not keep the dirt out of our house. It sifted through the fine cracks in the log walls and found its way into everything. Multiple times a day I wiped the grit from the kitchen table. I gave up trying to keep the cement floor clean. And before crawling into bed each night I removed the top blanket, stepped out the door, and shook the fine sand from its surface.

At times I felt closer to the earth than I ever wanted to be; it clung to my clothes and was hard to wash out of my hair. Even my teeth felt gritty after a walk to the pump for water. Not wanting to increase my hand-laundry burden, I allotted myself two skirts and two t-shirts to wear each week. On top of everything else, at certain times the water supply was so strained that local springs ran low, making any clothes-washing nearly impossible.

My daily bathing routine consisted of one or two gallons of water heated and poured into a plastic shower bag made for camping. It was a great luxury, but was limited in the level of miracle it could work. We had one small mirror which hung against a log wall in a shadowy alcove of our house. I used it to comb my hair each morning but quickly found there was little use dwelling on the image reflected there. I couldn't do much to improve it, so I tied a bandana over my hair, Tarahumara-style, and focused on life. On family. On work. On friends and neighbors.

But I gradually found myself succumbing to the conspiracy of the common, choosing to see only the unlovely and speaking negatively to myself. "Why even bother?" I would mutter under my breath as I contemplated sweeping the floor yet again or attempting to make my kids look presentable. Why, I wondered, should I try to improve our living conditions when everyone around us struggled similarly, usually wore soiled clothes, and certainly smelled worse than I did. Why care? What did it matter? I even began to question our presence in the village, thinking to myself, *Things will never change here; there's no hope for this place.*

One morning in early June at the peak of the dry season, just before the arrival of the summer monsoon rains, my 11-year-old-daughter Kristen came in the door from playing outside, hand held behind her back. "Mom," she said, "do you want to see what you look like to me?"

Before I could answer, she extended her clenched hand, holding out to me a single purple flower, one of the first brave blooms to appear before the rains, an exquisite symbol of tenacious beauty. Unable to speak, I wrapped my arms around her and held her tight.

In that instant it all became clear. Everything the world conspires against us is all bluster and bluff. Its accusations, its harsh assessments, its labels of *common* scrawled across everything holy, are all entirely false and hollow.

For what called out to me from that singular striking blossom was the very thing that seemed to wobble so precariously in the depths of my own heart—a certainty that strength, beauty, and hope endure…and that *they matter*. I borrowed that day from the lonely purple flower to bolster my battered convictions and found myself standing a little straighter and perceiving my purpose in the world with a little more clarity.

Now I know. Whenever I find myself muttering *Why even bother? ...Who really cares? ...*or *What difference will it possibly make anyway?* I realize I've caved in to the conspiracy of the common. And instead I try to borrow from the eyes of an 11-year-old girl so I might see realities the world claims are not really there.

......

"...whatever is true, whatever is noble, whatever is right,
whatever is pure, whatever is lovely, whatever is admirable—
if anything is excellent or praiseworthy—think about such things."
Philippians 4:8

WHEN GOD IS SILENT

I raised and lowered the squeaky handle of the water pump. The water came in a trickle, filled a gallon jug half full, then dripped to a stop. Dry again. *Lord, the village desperately needs rain. There's barely enough water for drinking and cooking, bathing is hard, and washing clothes impossible.* Still the rain didn't come. We rationed water and skimped and waited. It was six long weeks before the first drops fell.

In the middle of the night we were startled from our sleep by the sounds of angry shouting. A woman screamed and footsteps thudded past our house. My heart pounded as I realized that our neighbors, Manuel and Maria, were in another drunken rage. Maria would likely be badly hurt again. *Could we be an instrument of healing in this family, Lord? Please transform Manuel and Maria with Your love.* We talked to them, and loved them, and prayed for them. Yet the horrible fighting and abuse continued.

Another day, another familiar sight: a man looking timidly in our window, a woman with a baby standing behind him. Knocking on doors is culturally awkward; it is better to wait to be noticed. The baby was seriously ill. Could we drive them to the hospital? During the six-hour round trip on rutted dirt roads and for days afterward we prayed. *Please restore this little one to health, Lord, and in the process demonstrate Your love to this couple who don't know You.* But the child returned to the village in a small pine coffin, and we never saw the parents again.

Sometimes God is silent. Sometimes prayer is a lonely vigil. My heart is tuned to embrace God's emphatic "Yes!" but it doesn't leap to receive His whispered "No." Yet from the heart of the same Father issue both replies. I do not know why God answers as He does. Yet He is the Sovereign One, the One who sees what I cannot, the One who is weaving your life and mine into the fabric of His will.

Receiving "no" for an answer perhaps has the result of changing most profoundly the heart of the one who prays. God has used unanswered prayer to expand within me a view that embraces eternity, or if I cannot gain that, a more implicit trust in the One whose perspective is "too lofty for me to attain." (Psalm 139:6) In the process He has revealed much to me about Himself and about myself, and I have come away with a deeper appreciation for the heart of the Creator.

Thank you, Lord, for the immeasurable privilege of approaching You in prayer. Help me to receive with equal grace your "yes" and your "no," acknowledging that your goodness is demonstrated generously in both.

......

"By day the Lord directs his love, At night his song is with me—
A prayer to the God of my life." Psalm 42:8

CRICKET SONG

With each night the chorus of crickets grew, perhaps in praise for the rains. Whatever the cause, I was glad for it. No matter where I am, a cricket song reassures me in the darkness and steadies the ground beneath me. In a new and strange place it is a whisper from God assuring me He is everywhere present. I know for a fact that crickets in Mexico sing the same song as those in Africa and Canada and Michigan. What a wonder.

One night after John returned from a trip to town, he and I sat around the kerosene lamp at the kitchen table, enjoying the mail he brought. We had no internet in our remote location, and letters were a much-longed for, though infrequent, treat. We were hungry for reports from family and friends, always hoping the mail would bring only good news, but never sure what we would find.

In that night's batch came two letters with facts that seemed disjointed and at odds with one another, as if the pieces of information went zinging off in different directions, never to be reconciled. In the first, a dear friend told of her son's week at Bible camp and his receiving Camper of the Week award. In the second, an advisory from our mission stated we were not allowed to be in Mexico during the upcoming elections several months distant. The political climate was becoming unstable, and we were told to be alert to the possibility of terrorist activities in the Tarahumara area.

In the circle of light cast by the kerosene lamp two worlds collided, one that was safe and secure and another unstable and frightening. It all seemed so incongruous. How could

Campers of the Week and political terrorists live on the same planet? And why, oh why, were we living in proximity to the latter rather than the former?

And there it was, laid bare before our troubled hearts, the age-old question of risk and the dominion of God. Is He or isn't He able to supersede, and be trusted with, the circumstances of our lives? Does He or doesn't He call us to take risks for the sake of His beautiful Kingdom? I believed the answers to those questions were *He is* and *He does*, but my mother-heart still wanted to gather my kids and head back to the land of the Camper of the Week.

Risk is embedded—in varying degrees—in all of life. Flying in an airplane, traveling at high speeds in a car, rubbing shoulders with strangers in crowded places…all contain a degree of risk. And in many parts of the world people live under circumstances that call for great measures of courage just to get out of bed in the morning (or go to bed at night). Their lives are pressed upon even while they do ordinary things.

In order to serve others, some leave places of peace and prosperity for areas of danger. The Kingdom of God, ever growing on this earth, requires faith and daring on the part of simple Christ-followers to expand its reach. It requires counting the cost and deeming the reward greater than the risk. It requires a sober affirmation that there are no guarantees, yet God *can* be trusted.

Our risk was, in reality, minimal compared to that of many far braver souls the world over. No matter how I perceived the risk, however, I had to acknowledge that my arms would never be big enough or strong enough to protect my children. Never. No matter where we were.

Whatever threat any of us faces, whatever Kingdom risk we dare embrace, there is only One who has arms that are impenetrable, only One who is completely invincible.

He is the One whose name the crickets sing, the One who whispers reassurance in unexpected ways and places. He is the Everywhere-Present-One, the One whose dominion is without end.

......

"His dominion is an everlasting dominion that will not pass away, and his kingdom is one that will never be destroyed."
Daniel 7:14

SOME THINGS STAY WITH YOU FOREVER

The summer rains rumbled over the mountains and my spirits lifted. The barren brown fields sprouted grasses and wildflowers, and corn grew in patchwork plots that flowed up and down the hillsides. The ever-present dust was washed from the air and the world seemed to sparkle. A morning mist often hovered over the valley below, and when the sun burned it off a world of lush green was revealed. The transformative power of water was stunning.

The rain transformed not only the landscape, but also the people. Six weeks earlier they had walked behind tired horses, plowing parched, dusty soil and planting hardy native corn. In the miraculous cycle of life, the corn sprouted and waited, the people watched and waited, and when the first drops of rain fell from the sky it was as if the entire world, human and otherwise, breathed a deep sigh of relief. People looked younger, children seemed cleaner, our surroundings appeared more hospitable. Perhaps it was all because the powdery dust was finally washed from the creases of our faces, from our clothes, from our feet, and from our simple houses.

I embraced this season with passion and spent as much time outdoors as possible. I loved to wander the worn footpaths, now a network of inviting trails that wound through patches of wildflowers and deep green cornfields. I often set out to visit Tarahumara women, my children trailing along gathering bouquets of bright blooms.

On just such a day, I ended up at the home of Margarita, a Tarahumara woman with whom I felt a kinship. Margarita had an ample figure and a round face that usually bore a smile,

PASCHAL

defying her hard life. Her long black hair fell in a braid down her back, and her head was covered with a bright kerchief tied behind her neck.

I found Margarita in the hard-packed dirt yard behind her small house, children, dogs, and chickens scattered around. She was seated on a stump. In preparation for making a batch of tortillas, she was breaking off the dried kernels of corn from whole ears she had stored throughout the winter. On an open fire nearby, a pot of pinto beans bubbled, their earthy fragrance floating on the breeze.

Margarita smiled, and I extended my hand to her. Our fingers touched lightly, and she nodded her head almost imperceptibly to a nearby rock. I sat on it.

While her children and mine eyed one another warily, finally finding common ground in a nearby litter of puppies, she and I talked. We talked about our children's health. We talked about what our husbands were doing that day. We talked about how tall the corn was and about the rain. And then, in the midst of the mundane, Margarita unexpectedly slid the conversation into the realm of the profound by painting a word picture so exquisitely simple and beautiful that it squeezed my heart until it hurt.

I had asked what she'd done yesterday, and she described how she and her three youngest sons had climbed to the place where the large rocks behind her house flatten into a solid stone mesa pocked with large depressions. These depressions brimmed with rainwater, and in plain words she described how the sun shining all day on the black rock left large pools of warm water. It was here she bathed her little boys she told me. And washed her hair. In basins of clean, warm rainwater sparkling in the sun. Then they all stretched out on the slabs of hot rock until they dried. She looked up from her work. "It was very nice," she said, something in her dark eyes adding depth to her understatement.

I caught my breath, so riveted was I by the magnitude of beauty she had just portrayed—a harsh landscape that harbored pools of grace, the wet brown bodies of her young children splashing in sun-warmed water, the heat of black rock seeping into them as they stretched out upon the ground, the difficulty of daily existence melting away in the presence of this serendipitous provision. In her astonishing picture all the needs and longings of humanity suddenly merged with the breathtaking gifts of our gracious God into one defining metaphor.

Where the conversation went from there I cannot remember, for Margarita's description settled over me and began to shape me. What she (a woman who hauls water from a hand pump to heat over a wood fire in order to bathe her children in a galvanized bucket on a dirt floor) described to me in that moment was a gift—both to her and me—of great simplicity and lavish grace. It somehow took root in me and has never let go.

Some things stay with you forever. Summer rains. Wildflowers. Beauty shared across culture. And warm pools of rainwater there for the taking.

......

"Every good and perfect gift is from above…" James 1:17

SHEER EXTRAVAGANCE

Last night I counted the flickering of eight campfires in the valley below. People have moved life outside their small houses and do as much as possible in the pleasant summer air, cooking, eating, and visiting with each other. Each night births more fireflies, and the sight of them dancing in the dusky evening is like a smile on the face of the tired world.

This morning I discovered a hummingbird nest in the pine tree near the outhouse. I dragged a ladder to the tree and climbed it to peek over the edge of the tiny nest, which was woven of fine grasses and lined with fluff. Nestled inside were two eggs, each the size and color of a navy bean, miniscule parcels of promise. This, too, is a smile.

The wildflowers have sprung to life in the bounty of summer rains that now wash over the mountains. Reds, yellows, blues, and whites dot the fields of green. Loveliness, having been so long suppressed by drought and wind, seems to have burst out with abandon now that some rain has splashed upon the earth in a gentler season.

Chavela came by with some tamales, Tarahumara-style tamales with no filling, just solid corn dough. She invited me to pick *kelites*, wild greens that sprout among the cornfields during rainy season. We wandered far down the valley, and when we had picked enough we sat in the grass and talked and watched big black thunderclouds pile in heaps on one another. Beauty comes sometimes and sneaks up on you, in the plain and ordinary.

I hiked once to an alpine lake in Colorado on a July day not so different from those among the Tarahumara. Thunderclouds gathered and spit on my family and me. Tall grasses waved around our legs. But most extraordinary were the wildflowers, a staggering array of beauty that attested to the nature of God. For there, on a remote trail in a hidden corner of the earth, was a completely unrestrained offering, blossoms of stunning intricacy and varied color. Far beyond the scope of practicality or reason, the bounty overflowed into the realm of excess, of immoderation, an outrageous display made all the more questionable by the fact that few eyes will ever see it.

Those Tarahumara thunderclouds, that alpine meadow, and a thousand other experiences of sheer extravagance have come to define my God. He is excessive in nature, painting the landscapes of our lives with strokes of liberality, lavishing not only incomprehensible beauty on us, but also incomprehensible, undeserved grace and love.

And to think, this is *only* the beginning.

......

"No eye has seen, no ear has heard, no mind has conceived what God has prepared for those who love him…"
1 Corinthians 2:9

LOVING THE UNLOVELY

A small steel hook-and-eye latch secured the homemade screen door against the buzzing flies that threw themselves relentlessly against it. It also kept out my tiny neighbor. Three-year-old Abel had found his way across the field and stood peering into my small kitchen, face pressed hard into the screen.

Last week, in the middle of a downpour, some of our Tarahumara neighbor children came in with our kids to find a dry place to play. Abel came with them. Abel is one of the most unkempt and undesirable-looking children I have ever seen. He wore dirty sleeper pajamas cut off at the ankles. From playing in the puddles he was mud up to his knees, and his bare feet were caked with it. His face, always a crusty mixture of dirt and dried mucus, had a fresh stream of green stuff flowing from his nostrils to his mouth and beyond. His dark brown hair stood straw-like in all directions, and his pajamas reeked from the many times he had soiled himself.

In spite of all this, he conducted himself with the abandon typical of a three-year-old. He defied my attempts to confine him to a quiet activity and touched whatever he could reach in my kitchen. He glanced downward at his legs as a wet trickle emerged from the cut-off pajamas and puddled on my floor. He repeatedly asked for things I couldn't decipher. He climbed up on a kitchen chair and spread the filth from his nose all over the table with finger-painting motions.

And all the while he smiled at me. He smiled as if he thought himself irresistible. His dark eyes almost disappeared in crinkles as he grinned and babbled incoherently, turning his dirt-encrusted face to me as if I were a smitten admirer. It became almost more than I could bear. I tried not to look at him or speak to him, afraid I would unwittingly communicate what was so strongly welling up inside—the feeling that he was some kind of vermin I should sweep from my kitchen.

When the rain let up, I shepherded him to the door and told him it was time to go home. Then I got a bucket, a rag, and a big green bottle of *Pinol* and scrubbed until my kitchen reeked of pine oil.

Now here he was again, rubbing the thick stream of green goo from his nose all over the lower half of my screen door. The footless pajamas had been exchanged for an equally dirty t-shirt and ragged pair of jeans. He chattered at me. I ignored him. His smell floated in on the morning air.

He banged on the screen, and being afraid he would tear it, I turned around. He uttered a stream of incomprehensible words and turned his beaming face up to me as if basking in the strength of our great friendship. I couldn't bring myself to close the heavy wooden door in his face, but I turned my back on him and continued working until, finally, I could hear him turn and pad away toward home.

Watching his grimy figure disappear down the path, I took a deep breath of relief and was just exhaling when from somewhere deep inside came the words of Jesus. *Whatever you did not do for one of the least of these, you did not do for me.*

I recoiled at the thought of my stingy love for Abel representing the measure of my love for Jesus. I cringed to realize the begrudging grace I extended to my dirty little neighbor became the meager goodness I extended to Jesus. And tears welled up as I recognized in that ragamuffin child the spirit of my loving Lord, who shows no revulsion, but who, with boundless generosity, receives all the unlovely ones, all the unworthy ones, all the broken ones—like me.

......

"They also will answer, 'Lord, when did we see you hungry or thirsty or a stranger or needing clothes or sick or in prison, and did not help you?' He will reply, 'Truly I tell you, whatever you did not do for one of the least of these, you did not do for me.'" Matthew 25:44-45

BLUE IS THE COLOR

Where I come from blue is the color of Lake Superior's vast and frigid waters; it is the color of wood violets and forget-me-nots, and the color of noisy jays that scold from the shadows of pine boughs. It is not the color of corn.

Corn, where I come from, is yellow or white or a speckled mix of both. It's something we plunge briefly into boiling water, then eat dripping with butter and sprinkled with salt. Corn is not blue. Unless, of course, it is dried and bound into decorative bundles for autumn displays. But that hardly counts as *real* corn.

But real corn, I was to discover, is a far cry from the hybridized grocery store variety I knew. Real corn survives the drought and cold of the mountains in which I was now finding myself. The seed for real corn is saved from year to year and passed from generation to generation. Real corn forms the nutritional foundation of entire cultures and comes in a rainbow of spectacular colors—deep yellow, orange, red, brown, and, yes, blue.

I loved the varied colors of hardy corn that grew in the valley surrounding my house, and I loved the thick corn tortillas our neighbors would bring us, fragrant and steaming, wrapped in a scrap of cloth. They were made from dried whole kernel corn that had been soaked and cooked with lime, then ground with a small steel hand-crank mill that clamped to a wooden table. This ground meal was then finished on a stone *metate*, the mash being worked back and forth with a smooth hand-held stone, which from years of use fitted perfectly into the hollow of the larger rock. Patted into perfect rounds a quarter-inch thick, the tortillas were then cooked directly on the flat surface of an upright 55-gallon metal barrel that had been converted to a woodstove.

My favorite beyond all, however, were the blue corn tortillas. Fresh from the barrel stove, they were crisp on the outside, flecked with browned or blackened spots, and chewy on the inside. Their earthy aroma was as full of substance as was their hearty texture. They transformed a bowl of pinto beans into a feast and went equally well with a cup of coffee or all by themselves. Blue corn tortillas became synonymous with goodness and expectation.

One sunny late summer day I headed down the trail to Rufina's house. A short, rounded woman, Rufina had an 11-year-old son, Jacinto, who had a severe mental handicap, as well as physical deformities that forced him to walk on uneven legs with his permanently-bent arms held high. Jacinto wandered the valley freely, going from house to house, and often showed up at ours. His speech was difficult to understand, and he quickly became frustrated when he could not make himself clear, sometimes becoming violent. I usually assumed he was asking for a treat and gave him a flour tortilla or a piece of homemade bread.

Some people made fun of Jacinto, elbowing one another when they saw him coming, and speaking to him in exaggerated voices. Rufina sometimes laughed along, but her eyes revealed her pain. These remote mountains were a hard place to rear a needy child; there was no special education, nor any orthopedic specialist who could fit crooked legs with braces. The paths were uneven, and Jacinto often stumbled and fell, crying out in his pain and humiliation. Beyond the caring and kindness of neighbors, there was little support for this hurting family.

Rufina had appeared at our door on several occasions leading a small donkey loaded with firewood for sale. We were always glad to see her and were happy to bolster our woodpile as well as her enterprising spirit. Today I was paying a friendly visit, an attempt to discover more about the people and community that surrounded me and, specifically, to get to know Rufina better.

When I entered her littered yard I called out the common Tarahumara greeting—*"Cuiraba!"* She poked her head through the open doorway of her small log house and smiled, then shyly motioned me inside. The house was unkempt, with empty cans, their ragged lids still half attached, scattered over the dirt floor. She swooshed a cat from its scavenging among the pile of unwashed dishes on the small kitchen table and offered me a crudely-made wooden chair nearby.

Rufina sat on a chair alongside the wall near the door. Although Jacinto was not around, there were visual reminders of him in the one-room house—a small red jacket hanging from a nail by the solitary window and a tattered pair of children's shoes on the floor near the door.

A chicken had followed me into the house and began scratching under the kitchen table for food scraps. On another small table opposite me I noticed a large basket full of blue corn tortillas, a mass of fat flies buzzing above and crawling over them. I knew those flies also had access to the human and animal excrement that dotted the fields just outside the door. A fire blazed in the barrel stove and a pot of beans bubbled ferociously. The combination of the heat and visual images was stifling, and I desperately wished we were sitting on a log outside instead of sweltering in the tiny house.

Rufina and I were three languages apart. She spoke mainly Tarahumara. I spoke mainly English. So after I exhausted my Tarahumara vocabulary we fumbled around in Spanish, which I knew far better than she did. Then Rufina resorted to the universal language of hospitality and reached for the basket of tortillas, swishing the crawling mass of flies away in the same movement.

She held it out to me and smiled. *Eat*, she said. I felt the scene freeze momentarily and wondered if perhaps the earth had skidded to a stop in its circle around the sun. I wrestled through the philosophical implications of declining her offer and the digestive ramifications of accepting it, and in that warp of time that feels like eternity but is only a split second, graciousness won, and I reached out and took a tortilla.

I held it uncertainly for a moment then suddenly remembered it was common practice to heat tortillas before eating them. Instantly thankful for the overheated barrel stove, I stood and walked casually to it, then while chatting about something unrelated, I prayed a silent prayer and firmly pressed each side of the tortilla to the scorching surface.

Rufina smiled shyly as I sat back down, breaking the hot tortilla in two and telling her how much I love blue corn. The tortilla was dry, whether from hours of sitting uncovered in the basket or from my zealous attempts at ridding it of pathogens, but I never let on and ate the whole thing.

Sitting with Rufina, surrounded as we were by the stark realities of her life, it was obvious that even though Jacinto was out wandering somewhere in the valley, he was unmistakably embedded in the fiber of who she was. Her pain was written in the lines that marked her face. It was reflected in the weary sadness that saturated her eyes and was seen in the prematurely gray hair that escaped her kerchief. Here within the crude walls of her own home, the brave, carefree demeanor she often exhibited bore obvious cracks, minute fissures through which her grief seeped as if the greatness of it could not be contained.

I left Rufina's house that day both profoundly sad and cautiously encouraged. Sad for the enormous weight of pain we parents bear for our hurting children. Encouraged to sense the small beginnings of friendship with Rufina. And though I reasonably could have, I did not get sick.

Blue, I realized, is not only the color of big lakes and corn tortillas. In all its subtle variations of light and dark, it is to me also the dusky color of perplexity that defines our human experience. It is the cool color of measured risk required to extend ourselves to others. It is the deep-as-sky color of determination that drives steadfastness in suffering. It is the weighty, complex color that marks our shared pain in this world.

Living within this bewildering palette of human emotion, from brooding midnight blue to bold azure blue to the delicate delight of robin's egg blue, we are startled to find in ourselves both an uncommon strength and a terrible weakness. Even when our wild struggle to understand fails us, God's unfailing love is the full-spectrum rainbow that arches over all, and underneath are the everlasting arms. I know. For that is exactly where I once found myself, in the days before, and the weeks, months, and even years after I buried my own baby girl.

The One who created each hue and in infinite wisdom allows the subtle variations of dark and light into our lives tenderly and persistently invites us to find ourselves in Him.

For it is only in the fullness of *His* sacrificially broken heart that our own broken hearts find healing.

......

> "The Lord is close to the brokenhearted and saves those who are crushed in spirit." Psalm 34:18

A TWO LEPTA LIFE

A faint light flickered from the windows of Giltro's house. A modest adobe structure perched atop a small hill and surrounded by cornfields, Giltro's home and its light offered the only relief from the blackness that enveloped the length of the valley. As we bumped along the road on our midnight return to the village, my eyes were drawn to the pale glow that emanated not only from the windows but also from the cracks and crannies that had formed between the mud bricks.

A slight young man with a wife and 4 children, Giltro's simple life was in no way noteworthy. His friends and neighbors called him *Pulga*, or Flea, a nickname perhaps assigned in childhood, owing to his small frame. He didn't seem to mind the title, and played along with them, sharing jokes as well as serious conversations, all the while carving out his life within their midst. His face was quick to smile, a beautiful gesture that creased his eyes with deep lines that curved downward into his cheeks, in spite of his youth.

When asked to shepherd the small group of Christ-followers in his community Giltro agreed. He looked at the education he did not have, at the training he'd never received, and the task that was larger than he was. And he gave what little he had. On quiet nights, long after the plowing or planting or harvesting was done, he huddled in the candlelight, poring over Words that gave him life, hoping they would impart the same to others.

When asked to join the group of Tarahumara men and women from several communities translating the Bible into their language Giltro said yes. He looked at his inexperience, his lack of time, and the task that was bigger than he was. And he gave what little he had.

Through plentiful harvests and poor, through seasons of sickness and seasons of strength, whether the litter of pigs was large or pitiful, the hens were laying generously or not, and even when his donkey was struck and killed by lightening he got up every morning and went quietly, faithfully about his life.

When his precious wife, in resignation to long years of depression, slipped a rope around her neck and ended it all, Giltro staggered under the gut punch. And while the air was knocked out of him, hope remained within him. He looked at what he didn't have—a mother for four children, a companion in his labor, answers to hard questions—and the task that was bigger than he was. And he gave what little he had.

Long ago, as Jesus and His disciples watched people put offerings into the temple treasury, what seemed to be an ordinary act was shown to be a paradox of faith. Many rich people threw in large amounts. But a poor widow came and put in two very small copper coins (two *lepta*), worth only a fraction of a penny. "Calling his disciples to him, Jesus said, 'I tell you the truth, this poor widow has put more into the treasury than all the others. They all gave out of their wealth; but she, out of her poverty, put in everything—all she had to live on'" (Mark 12:41-43).

Out of his want, Giltro gave. The church he pastors stills gathers faithfully. The translation committee has translated the New Testament into the Tarahumara language. God brought another woman to be his wife and help raise his children. He took his two copper coins and reverently offered them. Overlooking all he didn't have, he gave what little he did have. And he, out of his poverty, has undoubtedly given more than many others.

I want to live like my brother Giltro, with a faith-filled generosity and an eye for what, by all reasonable standards, should never be.

I want to live a two-lepta life.

......

"Do not store up for yourselves treasures on earth, where moth and rust destroy, and where thieves break in and steal.
But store up for yourselves treasures in heaven, where moth and rust do not destroy, and where thieves do not break in and steal.
For where your treasure is, there your heart will be also."
Matthew 6:19

I WON'T BE HERE WHEN YOU GET BACK

Each time we got ready to leave the village for a few weeks, I would walk the winding path down the valley to Inez's house to say good-bye. When, after visiting awhile, I'd get up to go, she would invariably say, "I won't be here when you get back."

"Where are you going?" I would tease.

"Soy viejita!" (I'm an old woman!) she would reply. "Not much time left!"

I would grasp her work-worn hands and smile into her deeply creased face, searching her dark eyes for the twinkle that was always there. Then I would slip away, glancing over my shoulder to wave at the stooped figure with strands of coarse gray hair straying from her kerchief.

Upon returning to the village, I would take the familiar trail back to Inez's house. "Inez!" I would say. "You're still here!"

She would give a gap-toothed grin and chuckle. "So I am."

This went on for years, and even after we moved back to the U.S. the same exchange occurred whenever I visited.

Inez was one of the early Tarahumara Jesus-followers, having heard of the Savior in her middle years. Her son pastors one of the two small Tarahumara churches in the valley. Some of her grown children know and walk with Jesus, and some do not.

Inez worked hard into her late years, shuffling around in her shabby tennis shoes and fluorescent-orange socks, her calloused hands patting blue corn masa into perfect tortillas. She had no luxury in her life. Home consisted of mud walls and a dirt floor. A lone window allowed a beam of sunlight to penetrate the murky darkness. Summer and winter, the crude barrel stove crackled with flame as pot after endless pot of daily beans was simmered to tenderness. Her bed was a plank surface with a thin, lumpy mattress if she was fortunate, a mere padding of old blankets if she wasn't so blessed. No Posturepedic comfort for her old bones.

Inez could not read. The mystery of picking up the Bible and having God speak to her through its words was one she never knew. Her knowledge of the Word was limited, but her faith was simple and strong. She was a realist. Life was no picnic, but she didn't expect it to be. Somehow she knew something better awaited her. Unlike many of her people she did not fear death, but looked it in the eye with both a certainty of its coming and an unassuming confidence that because of Jesus she would prevail.

On one of his solo trips to Mexico, John emailed me after visiting the village. Inez had died, he told me, the day before his arrival. He had stayed on to attend her funeral.

Her body was laid to rest in a simple pine box made by her sons and grandsons. By hand, they planed the rough-sawn boards to make them smooth, then nailed them together—a simple cradle for her old body. They lined the coffin with her old clothes. The entire night before the funeral, Inez's body lay in state, the open pine coffin on the dirt floor of her kitchen, with family gathered around and candlelight warming the darkness.

Far from what the world would call "civilization," her frail bones are now buried in an unadorned graveyard at the foot of a hill. Her 89-year journey at an end, Inez's body lies cold, awaiting resurrection; but her spirit lives to behold wonders she never dared entertain nor could imagine.

The last time I saw her was several years ago. As I prepared to leave, she grasped my pampered American hands in her rough, leathery ones. She leaned into me and said matter-of-factly, "I won't be here when you get back." This time she was right.

......

"But we have this treasure in jars of clay…" 2 Corinthians 4:7

EVERYTHING ABOUT EVERYTHING

As they did for our neighbors, beans and tortillas fueled our days and satisfied our souls. They were a simple but succulent meal; we never tired of them. Just as some tortillas outshone others, so did some beans. Chavela's beans were hands down the best in the valley. Ask my children. Anytime I set out to visit Chavela, they begged to join me, hopeful that bowls of beans might somehow be in the picture. One day I learned the secret to her success, watching, fascinated, as she ladled scoop after scoop of pig lard from a large bucket into her pot of boiling beans. Their flavor was unsurpassed.

Chavela's house perched on a rocky hillside, just above an intermittent stream. She and I sometimes visited on the banks of that small stream as she washed clothes. Other days we sat on logs outside her house while she told me stories and, in her own unassuming way, taught me volumes about her life and people. She enlightened me with tales of the legendary trickster, coyote, and his schemes to deceive people. She shared about her people's deep fear of owls, harbingers of death, whose appearance in a tree near someone's home signaled the imminent demise of a family member. In moments of loneliness she bolstered me with the priceless gift of quiet friendship. Through our common language of Spanish she asked me questions and I asked questions of her. We laughed together, puzzled together, and sometimes could not quite figure out what one or the other of us was saying. She was a gift of inestimable worth to me.

Basking together in the sun one day as she wove an intricate belt on a handmade loom, a jet silently traced a ghostly path across the sky far above us. Pausing to stretch her arms, Chavela happened to glance upward. Then she looked at me, gave a quick nod toward the sky, and said, "Have you ever been in one of those?"

Rooted to her bare bones world as I was, the thought of flying across the great blue expanse above us in a barely visible speck of black seemed suddenly preposterous. I gave her a sheepish look, then forced myself to admit I'd done such a thing.

Chavela fingered some gray yarn she'd spun on a drop spindle from the fleece of her own sheep, then began weaving it into the design unfolding on her loom. In a moment she stopped, tipped her head to one side as she eyed me, and said, "You know everything about everything, don't you?"

In my best and calmest and yet most earnest way, I told her I didn't even come close to knowing everything. I really wanted to jump up and shout, to make perfectly clear to all the world the folly that had just been voiced. I was the learner here, the neophyte. I was the frequent fool in the company of these gifted people who knew how to carve out a life in an exceedingly hard place. And besides, I had lived long enough to have arrived at that dubious point of enlightenment where "the more I know, the more I know I don't know."

Despite my protests, I'm quite sure Chavela remained convinced of her perspective. In our limited understanding of one another in this world, it's too easy to layer misconceptions, one after the other, on top of reality.

And this was reality: John and I, over the course of some years, walked a wild learning curve among a people very different from us. But we simultaneously found ourselves treading a common path with those very same people, a path that wandered through the shared terrain of things loved and longed for, things dreaded, things dreamed. In the midst of daily life and laughter, language learning, development projects, and many conversations, Jesus was shared. He made Himself known to them and to us. He met all of us on the path and extended an invitation to newness in Him, to forgiveness, and to life that will never end.

I'm sure I was the one who learned the most—profound lessons about belonging, grief, rest, risk, treasure, beauty, and suffering. I sat not only at the feet of Chavela, but also Samuel, Rufina, José Luís, Berta, and even a dying dog and a stubborn cow. Life among the Tarahumara was difficult and costly, but it was also defining and rich. It was a gathering of grace, each experience heaped upon all the others until the impact of the beautiful, messy whole (as in all of life) far exceeded the sum of every little part. It was surely not about me or anyone else. It was only about Him who is our all in all—Creator, Redeemer, Upholder—He who is the first, the last, the beginning and end, the One who alone knows everything about everything.

......

"And God is able to make all grace abound to you…"
2 Corinthians 9:8

OUR TIMES ARE IN HIS HANDS

Family life in such an unusual place required we give up many things previously considered normal...things that had blended into the backdrop of life and hadn't seemed extraordinary. Things like running water, indoor toilets, electricity, libraries, schools, stores, parks, and playgrounds.

We attempted to adapt to our new environment while at the same time providing some of what was important from our old life. No libraries? We brought volumes of books to satisfy Kristen's voracious appetite for reading. No toy stores? We brought a "Goodie Box" chock full of craft projects, small toys, and new children's books that was only opened periodically, perhaps on rainy days or when boredom levels peaked. No parks or playgrounds? A reasonable hike from our house we discovered a beautiful stream with a sandy beach in a secluded pine forest and made it our own secret place. No electricity? We gathered around the small kitchen table at night, and by the light of a kerosene lamp were transported to other times and places as we read book after book aloud.

The kids became resourceful and soon were sledding down slippery pine needle-covered slopes with a piece of cardboard or flying kites made of plastic grocery sacks tied to a long string. They built shelves for their shared bedroom, fashioned pajama pegs from scrap wood, and even created a mousetrap, which was greatly needed but unfortunately didn't work. A swing John made and hung in the large pine tree by the outhouse became a gathering place not only for our kids but also for neighbor children.

Once a week we made pizza in the wood cook stove with carefully portioned-out American ingredients, and enjoyed the feast while listening to an episode of Adventures in Odyssey, feeling only grudgingly generous when we had to share a piece with Nemecio, our tall, smiling Tarahumara friend with an uncanny sense of timing.

What may appear to be an idyllic village life in reality paralleled the challenges of life anywhere. There were days that seemed golden and perfect, when everything was right in the world and we would have chosen to live nowhere else. There were other days when the weight of all they had left behind tipped the scales against the intrigue and newness of that place in our children's minds. They understandably longed for things we couldn't provide. We did our best to meet our children's needs while attempting to live out the grace and truth of Jesus among our Tarahumara friends. When we felt it best for our family, we left the village and John continued the work itinerantly. As is always true in an imperfect world, with that decision some challenges ended while others emerged.

No parent gets to the end and thinks *I did it all well.* Every parent, at one time or another, thinks *I would have done that differently if I knew then what I know now.* Many of us wish we could have given our children more, while others wish they hadn't given so much. Our choices allowed us to spend much time together as a family, to experience with one another the reality of another culture, to depend upon God in ways we could never have imagined. They also left our kids somewhat clueless about American culture, feeling awkward at times and on the outside looking in. As parents, we all set out on a path, try to self-correct along the way, and implore God to guide and fill in the gaps during the whirlwind days of child-rearing.

We'll never know what our family would have been like had we made other life choices. We only know who we are today. Our kids are honest about the challenges of that time, but they also speak to the unique ways the experience shaped them and of their ability to see the world differently now because of what they lived then.

Had I to do it over again of course I would do some things differently.

Had I to do it over again, *would* I do it over again?

Yes. I would.

......

"But I trust in you, O Lord; I say, 'You are my God.' My times are in your hands..." Psalm 31:14-15

A FINAL PRAYER OF DESPERATE FAITH

So I come on quiet feet, as if a Galilean child,
inching closer to the One who utters words of Life.

But in my hands there are no loaves, no fishes even.
Poor I come, bearing minnows only, and a crust.

Others follow, hungry all.
We eye the minnows and the crust, stomachs twisting,
trembling at our neediness.
Should we devour the paltry offering and run?

Or hold it out in foolishness and fear?

I let go the meager scraps
and feel my faith catch hard on terror's ragged edge.

Oh, come Lord Jesus! *Come!*

If You do not show up, we all go away hungry.
Famished.
More desperate than before for having dared to hope.

......

"…may your mercy come quickly to meet us,
for we are in desperate need." Psalm 79:8

> "Oh, to grace how great a debtor
> Daily I'm constrained to be..."

Come, Thou Fount of Every Blessing
Robert Robinson, 1735-1790

ABOUT THE AUTHOR

Anne Childs loves to find and cultivate beauty in the natural world and people around her. Through her years of work with those from Native cultures in the U.S. and Mexico she's been greatly enriched and has learned much about grace. One of her favorite things to do is spend time with her three grown children and their spouses, as well as with her seven beautiful grandchildren. She and her husband live in Flagstaff, AZ.

BOOKS FROM PEREGRINI PRESS

All hard copy editions are available wherever fine books are sold. All titles are also available as Kindle e-books to read on whatever digital device you prefer.

The Our Stories Series
Blue is the Color ~by Anne Childs
Far from Cold ~by Gillian Newham
Pursuit of a Thirsty Fool: 5 Years Down the Road and Still Thirsty ~by T.J. MacLeslie

The Field Notes Series
Forged on the Field ~Edited by T.J. MacLeslie
Voices from the Field ~ Edited by T.J. MacLeslie

Other Titles
Designed for Relationship – 5th Anniversary Edition (Autumn 2018) ~by T.J. MacLeslie
The Advent of Relationship ~by T.J. MacLeslie

Connect with us:
Email: info@peregrinipress.com
Web: www.peregrinipress.com
Twitter: @peregrini_press
Instagram: peregrini_press
Facebook: https://www.facebook.com/peregrinipress/

Made in the USA
San Bernardino, CA
23 September 2018